HAPPY BONSAI

Penguin
Random
House

Project Editor Jo Whittingham

Project Art Editor Louise Brigenshaw

Senior Editor Alastair Laing

US Editor Megan Douglass

US Consultant Mark Fields

Senior Jacket Creative Nicola Powling

Jacket Co-ordinator Lucy Philpott

Senior Producer (Pre-production)
Tony Phipps

Producer Francesca Sturiale

Creative Technical Support
Sonia Charbonnier

Managing Editor Dawn Henderson

Managing Art Editor
Marianne Markham

Art Director Maxine Pedliham

Publishing Director
Mary-Clare Jerram

Photography Nigel Wright
and Will Heap

Illustrations Peter Bull and
Debbie Maizels

DK India

**Assistant Art Editors
and Illustrators**
Adhithi Priya, Sonali Mahthan

Senior Art Editor Ira Sharma

Senior Managing Art Editor
Arunesh Talapatra

Senior DTP Designer Neeraj Bhatia

DTP Designer Manish Upreti

Production Manager Pankaj Sharma

Pre-production Manager Sunil Sharma

First American Edition, 2020
Published in the United States by
DK Publishing
1450 Broadway, Suite 801,
New York, NY 10018

A catalog record for this book
is available from the Library of Congress.
ISBN: 978-1-4654-9142-8

Printed and bound in China

A WORLD OF IDEAS:
SEE ALL THERE IS TO KNOW

WWW.DK.COM

HAPPY BONSAI

CHOOSE IT, SHAPE IT, LOVE IT

MICHAEL TRAN

Contents

Trident maple
Acer buergerianum
pp. 54–55

Amur maple
Acer ginnala
pp. 56–57

Japanese maple
Acer palmatum
pp. 58–59

Bougainvillea
Bougainvillea
pp. 60–61

European hornbeam
Carpinus betulus
pp.62–63

Cotoneaster
Cotoneaster horizontalis
pp.72–73

Lipstick fig
Ficus virens var. *glabella*
pp.80–81

Australian pine
Casuarina equisetifolia
pp.64–65

English hawthorn
Crataegus monogyna
pp.74–75

Japanese holly
Ilex serrata
pp.82–83

Japanese quince
Chaenomeles japonica
pp.66–67

Korean beech
Fagus crenata
pp.76–77

California juniper
Juniperus californica
pp.84–85

Hinoki cypress
Chamaecyparis obtusa
pp.68–69

Natal fig
Ficus natalensis
pp.78–79

Chinese juniper
Juniperus chinensis
pp.86–87

continued

Savin juniper
Juniperus sabina
pp.90–91

Dwarf crab apple
Malus spp.
pp.98–99

Japanese white pine
Pinus parviflora
pp.108–109

Rocky Mountain juniper
Juniperus scopulorum
pp.92–93

European olive
Olea europaea
pp.100–101

Ponderosa pine
Pinus ponderosa
pp.110–111

European larch
Larix decidua
pp.94–95

Ezo spruce
Picea jezoensis
pp.102–103

Scots pine
Pinus sylvestris
pp.112–113

Japanese larch
Larix kaempferi
pp.96–97

Mountain pine
Pinus mugo
pp.104–105

Japanese black pine
Pinus thunbergii
pp.114–115

Manila tamarind
Pithecellobium dulce
pp.116–117

Satsuki azalea
Rhododendron indicum cvs
pp.126–127

English yew
Taxus baccata
pp.134–135

Blackthorn
Prunus spinosa
pp.118–119

Sageretia
Sageretia thea
pp.128–129

Japanese yew
Taxus cuspidata
pp.136–137

Chinese quince
Pseudocydonia sinensis
pp.120–121

Coastal redwood
Sequoia sempervirens
pp.130–131

Chinese elm
Ulmus parvifolia
pp.139–139

English oak
Quercus robur
pp.122–123

Tamarisk
Tamarix chinensis
pp.132–133

Japanese elm
Zelkova serrata
pp.140–141

THE **BASICS**

Bonsai today

Bonsai has developed as an idealized representation of nature in miniature and is deeply rooted in Asian culture. The art of creating and maintaining a beautiful tree in a small pot requires care and skill, which are best learned by cultivating a bonsai of your own.

INNOVATION WITHIN A TRADITION

In Japan, design guidelines and styles have shaped a traditional philosophy, which tends to be followed wherever bonsai is practiced. However, with its increasing popularity in the West, bonsai has begun to evolve. While it remains essential to master classic techniques, tree species and natural landscapes from around the world are inspiring exciting new ways to shape and display trees.

Modern style

More about individuality than conformity, modern bonsai styles accept the natural growth habit of trees, often making them older and wilder in appearance. What would traditionally be considered aesthetic flaws are allowed to become part of a tree's character.

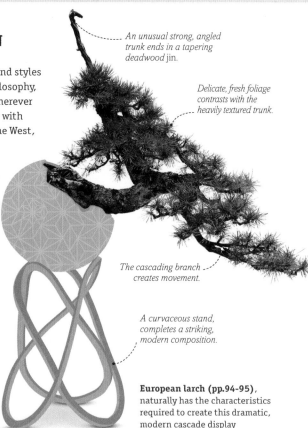

An unusual strong, angled trunk ends in a tapering deadwood jin.

Delicate, fresh foliage contrasts with the heavily textured trunk.

The cascading branch creates movement.

A curvaceous stand, completes a striking, modern composition.

European larch (pp.94-95), naturally has the characteristics required to create this dramatic, modern cascade display

Traditional style

A bonsai grown according to traditional guidelines reflects the form of a tree growing in nature. Its image will reflect one of the many clearly defined classical styles (see pp.22–23), although it is not essential to adhere to these rigidly.

The largest, main tree forms the focal point of the design

Smaller trees create an asymmetrical family group around the larger tree.

Traditional groups contain an odd number of trees of the same species

A classical shallow, oval pot forms an unassuming base.

Japanese larch (pp.96-97), recreates a natural grove in this traditional group

How your tree grows

A good grasp of the basic structure of your tree and how it functions helps give you a clear picture of how bonsai techniques work. With this knowledge, you can adapt care, pruning, and maintenance to your local climate and even individual trees.

SEASONAL ENERGY FLOW

Understanding the way energy flows around a tree helps time tasks correctly. When new leaves start to photosynthesize in late spring, energy levels rise, fueling summer growth and the formation of new buds for the following spring. Harness this energy during the "development" phase of young bonsai, to create a strong trunk and branch structure. In fall, energy is taken from foliage, and stored in the roots and vascular tissue, causing the trunk and branches to thicken. These resources are used for early spring growth, which swells the branches and trunk again, and leaves energy levels low. This is the time to carry out "refinement" of bonsai as they mature.

New growth saps energy in early spring

Blossom and new leaves on a dwarf crab apple

VASCULAR SYSTEM

This is the tree's transport system for water, minerals, and sugars, which lies hidden beneath the bark. A basic knowledge of its structure is useful to understand how a growing tree functions and will help you avoid causing damage during pruning and the creation of deadwood features.

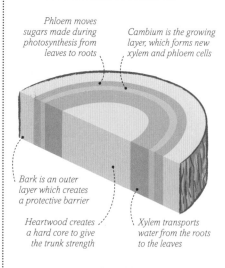

Phloem moves sugars made during photosynthesis from leaves to roots

Cambium is the growing layer, which forms new xylem and phloem cells

Bark is an outer layer which creates a protective barrier

Heartwood creates a hard core to give the trunk strength

Xylem transports water from the roots to the leaves

A cross-section of living wood

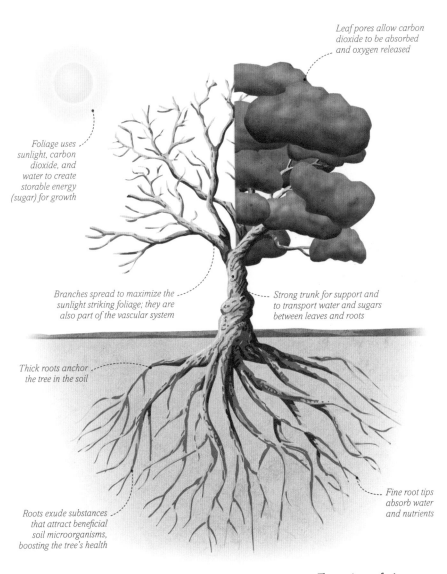

Leaf pores allow carbon dioxide to be absorbed and oxygen released

Foliage uses sunlight, carbon dioxide, and water to create storable energy (sugar) for growth

Branches spread to maximize the sunlight striking foliage; they are also part of the vascular system

Strong trunk for support and to transport water and sugars between leaves and roots

Thick roots anchor the tree in the soil

Fine root tips absorb water and nutrients

Roots exude substances that attract beneficial soil microorganisms, boosting the tree's health

The anatomy of a tree shows that each of its "organs" has to function well to keep it healthy. A small bonsai works in the same way as a mighty forest tree.

Obtaining a bonsai tree

Not every tree is equal in terms of bonsai. Make life easier
by starting with material that already exhibits some of the
characteristics you are looking for. This can save years of waiting
for a tree to grow to the desired size or shape.

BUYING A BONSAI OR PRE-BONSAI TREE

Ready-made bonsai are expensive, but you won't have to shape the tree or wait for it to grow. They are widely available online and from garden centers, but a specialist bonsai nursery will supply a good range of species and expert advice. Nurseries often also stock pre-bonsai. These cheaper, younger trees already have desirable features, but allow you to make your mark as they grow.

STARTING FROM NURSERY STOCK

Creating a bonsai from ordinary nursery trees and shrubs is an affordable and exciting way to begin. The process takes 3–10 years, depending on your goals and starter material. Select species with small leaves and choose plants with plenty of branches. A sturdy, unmarked, tapering trunk, and attractive *nebari* (root-flare) are also desirable, as these are difficult to alter.

A strong branch structure makes bonsai much easier

A pre-bonsai cypress tree

Dense branches will need pruning and wiring

Check for healthy roots that flare at the trunk's base

Junipers are good candidates for bonsai

YAMADORI—COLLECTED FROM THE WILD

Wild-collected (*yamadori*) trees, stunted and scarred by a lifetime in the mountains, were the original bonsai. Their unique characters can't be recreated, and they remain highly valued, but their care takes great skill, making *yamadori* unsuitable for hobbyists. Wild trees can only be collected with the correct legal consent. In places, it is illegal to uproot any plant without the landowner's permission.

············· *Ancient, gnarled deadwood is tricky to recreate*

Japanese yew, (pp.136–137)

RAISING FROM SEED

Starting from seed is the cheapest option, but may not be the best for beginners, because it does require knowledge, skill, and a lot of time. It takes about 30 years to create a medium-sized bonsai, so try it as a side project.

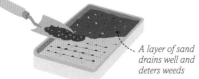

···· *A layer of sand drains well and deters weeds*

···· *Remove weak plants to create space for growth*

1 Check if seeds need specific treatment before sowing. Fill a seed tray with potting soil, add a layer of sand, and sow into rows. Top with sand and put outside.

2 After germination, thin out any seedlings growing close together by removing weaker plants. Leave outside to encourage strong roots and shoots. Water regularly.

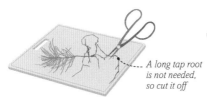

···· *A long tap root is not needed, so cut it off*

Plant seedlings into their own ··· pots to grow

3 After a year, lift each seedling from the tray. Spread the roots on a board and remove the central tap root. Lateral roots will grow on to form a *nebari* (root-flare).

4 Plant seedlings into small pots of potting soil, with coarse sand at the base. Once established, plant out into the soil for two years to allow vigorous growth.

Where to grow

Traditionally, bonsai are hardy trees and are grown outdoors. Their compact size makes them appealing house plants, but most will only flourish outside. If you want to grow bonsai in your home, check the tree profiles and choose a species that thrives indoors.

POSITION AND HUMIDITY

Finding the right situation for your tree in your garden or home will allow it to thrive. All trees occupy a specific habitat in nature, and replicating these environmental conditions as closely as possible is the key to success.

Sunlight

Provide full sun in early spring, although many deciduous trees are best kept under a shade cloth in summer, when the heat and intense sunlight can scorch their foliage. Conifers can tolerate full sun all year. Direct exposure to sunlight can also be harmful in winter, in combination with icy winds and freezing temperatures.

Air flow

Good ventilation is important to allow foliage to exchange gases or "breathe" and to prevent the stagnant air favored by fungal diseases. Allowing plenty of space between trees is usually enough for air to flow freely. The movement of leaves and branches in the wind also encourages compact growth and sturdier shoots.

Temperature

A tree's responses to the changing seasons are, in part, a reaction to natural temperature fluctuations between day and night, and throughout the year in a temperate climate. It is important that trees experience these natural variations—especially those grown indoors—to allow them a period of rest during winter dormancy and spur them into spring growth at the right time.

Check variations in temperature to keep trees happy

A maxima-minima thermometer

Humidity

Humidity in the air and morning dew are both important sources of water for many tree species growing in the mountains. Misting plants in the morning can help replicate this natural effect. Some tropical species come from humid climates and need regular misting in a dry, indoor environment.

GROWING BONSAI OUTSIDE

Most bonsai need to be grown outdoors to provide ideal growing conditions, similar to those in their native habitat. Choosing species to suit your local climate is the best way to ensure long term success.

• Keep bonsai on a bench in a garden, stand on a pole in a small space, or place on ledge on a balcony (see pp.124–125).
• Allow ample space between trees, to ensure good airflow and prevent them casting shade on each other.
• Place conifers in a south-facing spot with full sun year-round. Move deciduous trees to a shaded, north-facing position in summer.
• Move species that need protection from cold weather (see individual tree profiles) undercover for winter.

GROWING BONSAI INDOORS

Some tree species are tolerant of indoor conditions and can be grown as wonderful bonsai given the right care. The best choices are the natal and lipstick figs and Chinese elm.

• Position near a window, in bright natural daylight. Additional light from an LED grow light helps produce even growth.
• Raise humidity by misting, preferably in the mornings so the humidity evaporates completely over the course of the day.
• Keep trees away from direct sources of heat, such as vents.
• Avoid temperature drops when heating is turned off, especially for tropical species.
• Move deciduous trees to a cooler position in fall, to initiate winter dormancy.

Sunlight fuels growth, but can also be harmful

Leaving gaps between trees allows air to flow

Ideal outdoor conditions

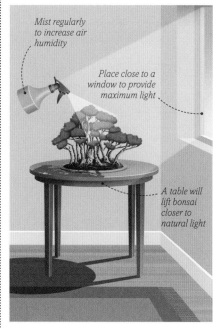

Mist regularly to increase air humidity

Place close to a window to provide maximum light

A table will lift bonsai closer to natural light

A good indoor environment

Choosing a pot

The marriage of a tree and pot is central to the art of bonsai, which means that selecting the perfect pot for your tree can be a challenge. There are many traditional rules to guide you, but always ensure the pot has adequate drainage holes in its base.

TRADITIONAL RULES FOR POT SELECTION

Only invest in a high quality pot once your tree has begun the refinement phase. As a rule, the width of the pot should equal two-thirds of the tree's height, and its height should match the diameter of the base of the trunk. Its shape, color, and texture should complement the tree. Rugged conifers are displayed in rough or angular pots, while deciduous trees are paired with smooth, curved containers.

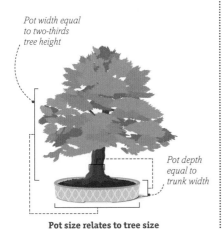

Pot width equal to two-thirds tree height

Pot depth equal to trunk width

Pot size relates to tree size

CLASSIC POTS

Bonsai pots are as complex and meaningful as the trees they contain. Traditionally, certain shapes are considered to have masculine or feminine qualities, which match the character of trees they will suit.

This unglazed, masculine pot has angular lines and a sturdy rim and feet

Brown, rectangular pot with rim

The height of this classic masculine shape provides stability for a cascade

Tall, white, hexagonal pot

A feminine rimless form in a plain color suits delicate deciduous trees

White, glazed, oval pot

Rounded edges, elegant feet, and a pastel glaze make this a feminine pot

Rectangular blue pot

Arched side walls add substance, which suits sturdy deciduous trees

Cream, glazed, oval pot

A feminine oval sets off rounded trees. Rims make pots appear wider

Turquoise, glazed, oval pot

MODERN POTS

Modern pots have a distinctive character and are derived from simple, often geometric shapes, with repetitive qualities, which suit modern styles of bonsai. They are not mass produced, but are available from bonsai nurseries and potters.

Geometric cuts and linear decoration create symmetry reminiscent of classical pots

Cubist lotus design

The slanting shape and rough finish suit a modern conifer cascade

Crescent-shaped pot

ROCKS

Rough and dark in color, the best rocks evoke mountain landscapes and have pockets for planting. Perfect forms are rare, so stones are shaped or made of composite materials.

Rugged, textured, with a natural form, this is an ideal rock

A suitable rock

Design principles

Many concepts, ideas, and rules influence bonsai design, covering the appearance of everything, from curves in the trunk, to branch position, and even the ideal front for viewing. These all play a role, but respect for each tree's unique character is the guiding principle.

BONSAI AESTHETIC

The creation of a sense of age is central to the art of bonsai. This is achieved by carefully working with each element of a tree, such as the root flare, fine branching, and small leaf size, to produce an air of maturity. The form chosen is also important and is influenced by established bonsai styles. The canopy can form a stable, symmetrical shape, or it may display more dynamic asymmetry, representing trees that have been molded by the elements. These rugged forms are traditionally described as masculine, and finer, more delicate trees as feminine. Although these terms may now seem outmoded, they offer a useful way to think about bonsai styling.

Feminine characteristics

Trees described as feminine are elegant, with smooth bark, no visible scars from cutting or wiring, and no deadwood. Light, airy foliage is borne from a fine structure of branches and highlights soft movement in the slender trunk. It is deciduous trees, with their bare winter branches, that most commonly exhibit these characteristics.

Masculine characteristics

Masculine trees are usually conifers, which impress with their compact, sturdy stature and dense pads of foliage on strong, gnarled branches. Their powerful trunks bear dramatic curves, deadwood, and deeply fissured bark, as signs that the tree has withstood the forces of nature.

ASYMMETRY AND THE GOLDEN RATIO

Young trees often grow symmetrically and gradually develop asymmetry as they mature. One goal when styling bonsai is to create asymmetry and with it a sense of age. The golden ratio (1:1.6) can be used to achieve this. So, if a tree's final height is to be 16 in (42 cm), divide this by 1.6 to find the length of trunk above the lowest branch (10 in/26 cm), which leaves 6 in (16 cm) of trunk below it.

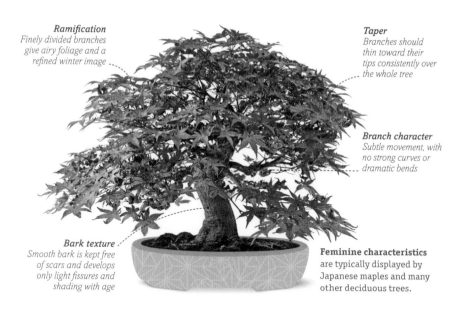

Ramification
Finely divided branches give airy foliage and a refined winter image

Taper
Branches should thin toward their tips consistently over the whole tree

Branch character
Subtle movement, with no strong curves or dramatic bends

Bark texture
Smooth bark is kept free of scars and develops only light fissures and shading with age

Feminine characteristics are typically displayed by Japanese maples and many other deciduous trees.

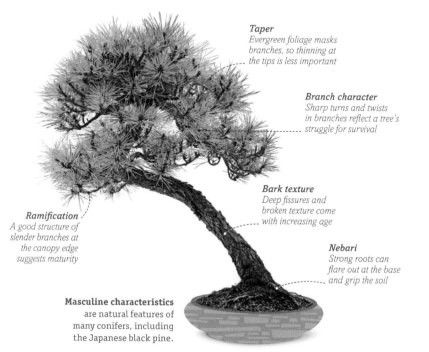

Taper
Evergreen foliage masks branches, so thinning at the tips is less important

Branch character
Sharp turns and twists in branches reflect a tree's struggle for survival

Ramification
A good structure of slender branches at the canopy edge suggests maturity

Bark texture
Deep fissures and broken texture come with increasing age

Nebari
Strong roots can flare out at the base and grip the soil

Masculine characteristics are natural features of many conifers, including the Japanese black pine.

Classical styles

Many traditional bonsai styles have been developed in Japan over centuries to represent idealized images of natural tree forms. Not all bonsai fit neatly into a single style, but they are valuable when planning the development of a young tree.

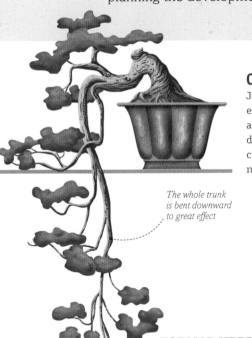

CASCADE

Japanese: *kengai*. This dramatic style embodies the struggle between a tree and the forces of nature, with a downward-growing trunk, strong curves, and deadwood. Conifers naturally lend themselves to this style.

The whole trunk is bent downward to great effect

Branches taper toward the tree's apex, but are never symmetrical

FORMAL UPRIGHT

Japanese: *chokkan*. This is the only bonsai style in which a straight trunk stands perpendicular to the ground. Trees are usually placed off-center in their pot. Beautiful in its simplicity, it is often overlooked for this reason.

INFORMAL UPRIGHT

Japanese: *moyogi*. A popular style, with gentle movement in the trunk and branches, to produce an appealing natural shape that is easy to appreciate. It is a good choice for beginners, and young bonsai are often available in this style.

The trunks of both trees have similar shapes

A smaller cluster of trees balances the dominant group

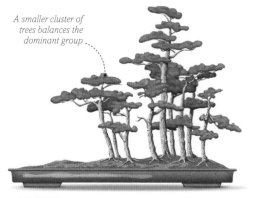

TWIN TRUNK

Japanese: *sokan*. Also often referred to as "father and son," this style features two different sized but harmonizing trees. Both trees have the same visual flow, with the larger one usually reaching a branch over as though to shelter its partner.

GROUP

Japanese: *yose-ue*. Evoking a wider landscape, these compositions of the same tree species are typically divided into a larger main group and accompanying small group. In the past, an odd number of trees was always used to avoid symmetry, but today the style is less prescriptive.

LITERATI

Japanese: *bunjin*. A simple, minimalist style, often regarded as one of the hardest to achieve. The focus is on the essence of the tree, which has a thin, elegant trunk clothed in old bark, with minimal branching and foliage.

A long, bare trunk is central to the literati style

Modern styles

The origins of modern bonsai styles lie in the West, where artists found it hard to fit native trees into classical Japanese styles. New styles have become established to work with the natural forms of these species, and also as a reaction against the traditional rules.

Small foliage requires classic skills to produce

Upright branches mimicking nature, are not normally seen in bonsai

White rocks from Europe are used in modern, but never traditional, styles

NATURAL

This was the first style to emerge outside Asia. Elements that would be considered "wrong" in classical bonsai are included to create the impression of a tree as it would be found in its natural habitat.

CANDELABRA

Inspired by the regrowth of alpine trees torn by high winds, in this style the leading shoot tips are removed, to be replaced by many surrounding branches, which shoot upward and form new, smaller apexes.

Branch tips resemble the arms of a candelabra

FAIRY TALE

This style embraces the features of ancient deciduous trees in Europe, such as bulky, scarred trunks, and deadwood, which are seen as undesirable in classical bonsai. This allows previously unusable trees to become beautiful bonsai.

A hollow trunk is perfect for the fairy tale style

Coiled branches exhibit bizarre and unnatural forms

BURTON

The Burton, or cosmic, bonsai style counters every classic rule and does not reflect natural growth. Instead, a complex, playful, twisting structure of branches and deadwood creates an almost surreal image of a tree.

Essential toolkit

Many specialist bonsai tools are available, each of which has been developed for a specific technique. There is no need to invest in them all immediately, however, because a basic set of tools will get you off to a good start as you learn to prune and care for your tree.

CLEANING TOOLS

Good plant hygiene is vital to keep trees healthy, which makes brushes and tweezers essential tools for removing dirt, algae, and dead leaves. They are also handy during repotting and the shaping and maintenance of deadwood.

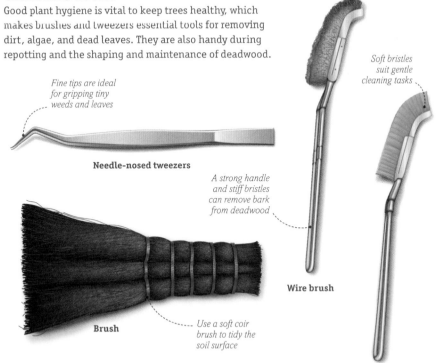

Soft bristles suit gentle cleaning tasks

Fine tips are ideal for gripping tiny weeds and leaves

Needle-nosed tweezers

A strong handle and stiff bristles can remove bark from deadwood

Brush

Use a soft coir brush to tidy the soil surface

Wire brush

Plastic brush

CUTTING TOOLS AND ACCESSORIES

Having quality tools and the right accessories on hand allows you to prune and shape your tree with ease. Tools come in both stainless and black, hardened steel. There is little difference, but hardened steel is easier to sharpen.

Use to cover pruning cuts for rapid healing

Cut paste

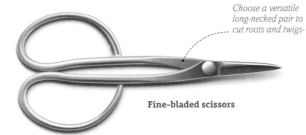

Choose a versatile long-necked pair to cut roots and twigs

Fine-bladed scissors

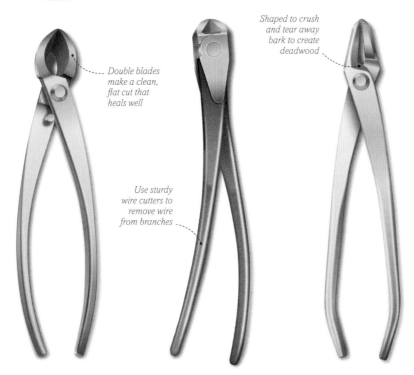

Double blades make a clean, flat cut that heals well

Shaped to crush and tear away bark to create deadwood

Use sturdy wire cutters to remove wire from branches

Concave cutters　　　**Heavy duty wire cutters**　　　**Jinning pliers**

✚ Potting up

Established bonsai remain in small pots, but still need regular repotting to refresh the soil at their roots, which degrades over time. Replenishing soil gives roots access to the water, nutrients, and air that are essential for the healthy growth of the entire tree.

WHEN TO REPOT

An healthy tree needs repotting the spring after it starts to become root-bound. Watch for soil drainage becoming poorer, roots appearing through the drainage holes, and the whole root ball starting to rise out of the pot. Repot deciduous species every 2–4 years and conifers every 4–8 years.

GETTING THE SOIL RIGHT

Special soil mixes are created to suit each tree species (see tree profiles). Components are used in varying proportions to create ideal conditions for roots. Akadama is a Japanese granular, clay-based material, which retains water. Roots grow through microscopic tubes in the clay, breaking down the particle size and encouraging further root development. A higher proportion of akadama is used to grow deciduous trees and less for conifers. Pumice is a pale, low density volcanic rock with many tiny pores, which is ideal for improving aeration. Lava is also porous and is added for aeration, but retains less water than pumice.

PREPARING THE POT

Clean the pot and put plastic mesh over the holes in the base, to let water and air through, but keep the soil in.

1 Cut a length of wire and twist to shape, so that the ends going through the hole fit tightly against its edges.

2 Cut plastic mesh to cover the hole. Push the two ends of the wire through the square of mesh.

3 Insert wire ends through the hole and fold against the pot base. For a neat finish, trim ends with wire cutters.

ANCHORING THE TREE

Firmly tying the tree to its pot helps create unity between the two so that they can mature together. This stability also allows healthy soil microbiology, and with it root growth, to establish undisturbed.

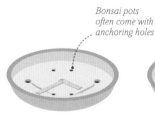

Bonsai pots often come with anchoring holes

1 Remove old soil from around roots with a chopstick. Prune roots (see p.48) and replace soil in one area of the root ball each time you repot. Use sharp scissors to make clean cuts.

2 Find thick structural roots or the strongest parts of the root system where the wire will be attached. Mark the holes in the pot closest to these roots, to show where the tie-down wires will go.

3 Once the holes to be used for anchoring have been chosen, use wire cutters to cut lengths of steel wire. Make two 90° bends in each wire to line up with the holes, so it will fit through them.

Trimmed wires are easy to hide

4 Push the wire through from the base, add an appropriate soil mix to the pot, and position the tree. Bend the steel wire over the tough part of the root and twist it to hold the tree in position.

5 Trim any excess wire away neatly with wire cutters to produce a neat and tidy finish. Repeat the process to tie down any other roots identified for anchoring.

6 Fill the pot with soil, gently pushing it among the roots with a chopstick. Hide the ends of anchor wires under the soil. Create an attractive soil contour and top dress with a thin layer of moss.

General care

The correct care is key to good plant health and success, particularly when trees are grown in small, shallow pots. Providing for a tree and understanding its daily needs are the foundations of bonsai, upon which the techniques to shape the tree are built.

WATERING

Use a watering can or hose with a fine nozzle to avoid disturbing the soil surface. Water soil evenly from all sides, until excess runs from the drainage holes. Use rainwater if possible, because the mineral content of hard tap water and chemically softened water can harm some species. Akadama soil changes from dark brown when wet, to light reddish brown when dry. This shift in color is usually a safe sign to water; check profiles for the needs of each species.

FERTILIZING

Apply a solid fertilizer monthly throughout the growing season. Use an organic feed to promote healthy roots and beneficial soil microorganisms. Fertilizers contain three main elements: nitrogen (N), phosphorous (P), and potassium (K). Bonsai generally need a balanced fertilizer with a roughly equal ratio of these main nutrients, shown by an N:P:K ratio of 5:6:5. Switch to a low-nitrogen feed (2:5:5) during refinement, when vigorous growth is not required.

Avoid splashing foliage to prevent fungal diseases

Blackthorn (pp.118–119)

Plastic covers protect fertilizer pellets from birds

Lipstick fig (pp.80–81)

SEASONAL CARE AND PROTECTION

The care that your trees need changes with the seasons. It is important to time tasks correctly and respond to different weather conditions throughout the year. This quick guide tells you what to do when.

Spring

Water more frequently and begin to feed as trees start to grow. Be wary of late frosts and protect trees if necessary. Check for weeds and remove promptly.

Summer

Water up to twice daily and use a shade cloth to protect deciduous trees from strong sunlight. Shade ceramic pots to stop them heating up and damaging roots.

Tweezers are ideal for picking out tiny weeds

Korean beech (pp.76–77)

Shade cloth keeps bonsai cool and out of intense sun

Cotoneaster (pp.72–73) and trident maple (pp.54–55)

Fall

Reduce watering and feeding as growth slows. Check for pests and diseases. Tidy fallen leaves, remove any dead branches, and clean bark and deadwood.

Winter

Reduce watering and stop feeding while trees are dormant. Place outdoor trees on the ground in groups to protect from cold, or move to a greenhouse, cellar, or garage.

A soft brush with plastic bristles cleans bark gently

Savin juniper (pp.90–91)

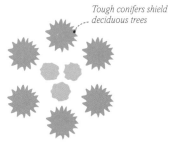

Tough conifers shield deciduous trees

Trees arranged to protect less hardy varieties in the center

Pruning to shape

Pruning is the technique used throughout all stages of bonsai development to direct a tree's growth. An understanding of the effects of pruning and how to execute cuts correctly will help you realize the potential of your tree.

HOW PRUNING WORKS

Removing shoot tips through pruning alters the balance of growth hormones in a branch, activating the growth of back buds, away from the growing tip. This creates finer branches, and also divides resources among more shoots, causing a reduction in both leaf size and the stem length between leaves (internode), all of which gradually refines the tree's image. Pruning between late spring and early summer, once spring shoots have hardened off (toughened and darkened), allows any foliage removed to be replaced by new growth from back buds.

TECHNIQUES AND TOOLS

Specialist tools have been created specifically for pruning bonsai. Use them correctly to avoid damaging your tree and to help it heal quickly.

1 Use concave cutters to remove branches. Cut flush to the trunk to continue its line. To shorten a branch, cut to leave a small stump above a bud.

2 Completely cover the freshly cut site with cut paste to seal it. This helps prevent infection, which could cause the surrounding tissue to die back.

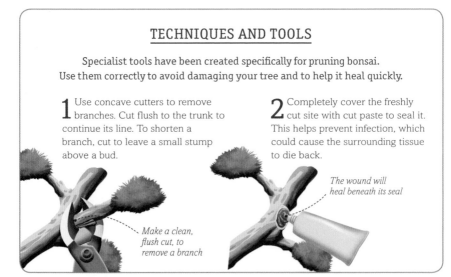

The wound will heal beneath its seal

Make a clean, flush cut, to remove a branch

THE DEFINING BRANCH

A tree's most characterful branch is known as the defining branch (or *sashi-eda* in Japanese). Often the longest or lowest branch, its direction and flow are followed by every other branch, making it key to any design. The form varies depending on the style of the tree: flowing downward in cascades and horizontally in upright styles. A defining branch can be an existing branch, chosen for its character, or can be shaped using pruning and wiring. Either way, establishing its tapering shape and movement is the first step in bonsai design.

BRANCH HIERARCHY

In order to describe a tree's structure clearly, different parts of a branch are given a named hierarchy in bonsai. Primary branches are the main structural branches that grow directly from the trunk; secondary branches arise from primary branches; and the finest tertiary branches are produced from the secondary branches.

Growth at the apex is styled to balance the sashi-eda

Short limbs opposite the sashi-eda *create good asymmetry*

Higher branches echo the defining branch's character

This tree's longest, lowest limb is its defining branch

A cascading Chinese juniper has a particularly long and dramatic defining branch.

STRUCTURAL PRUNING

Prune your tree early in its development to form its basic structure or "bones." Trees are shown with bare branches to aid understanding, but should be pruned when in leaf, to allow the cuts to heal quickly. Carry out structural pruning during summer. The goal is to improve the lines of the trunk and main character branches, and highlight their attractive features, such as curves or deadwood. Cut primary branches flush to the trunk on trees with feminine traits, or alternatively leave a stump to create a deadwood feature on more masculine conifer species.

"The goal of structural pruning is to improve the lines of the main branches and trunk."

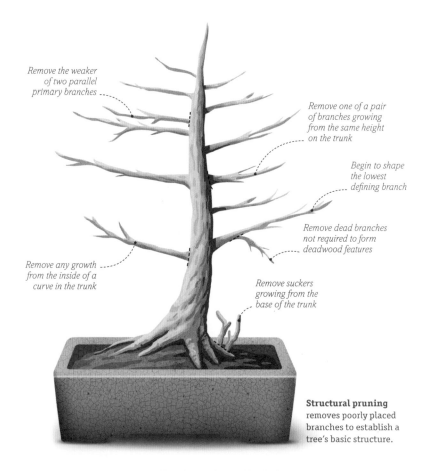

Remove the weaker of two parallel primary branches

Remove one of a pair of branches growing from the same height on the trunk

Begin to shape the lowest defining branch

Remove dead branches not required to form deadwood features

Remove any growth from the inside of a curve in the trunk

Remove suckers growing from the base of the trunk

Structural pruning
removes poorly placed branches to establish a tree's basic structure.

DEVELOPMENTAL PRUNING

As the tree develops, prune the secondary branches to continue the character of the primary branch they arise from and shape the tree further. Use concave cutters or scissors to remove branches growing in the wrong direction and ensure that only two branches originate from any single point on a primary branch. Prune in late spring or early summer, when shoots have hardened off (toughened and darkened), and the tree has energy to respond with new growth.

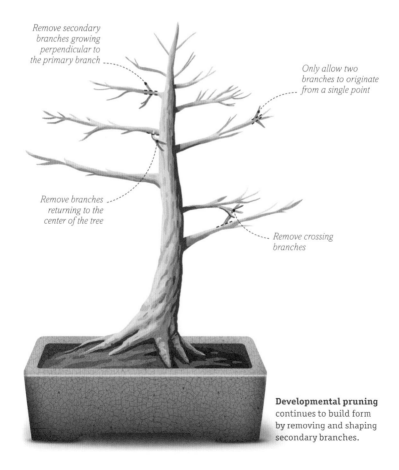

Remove secondary branches growing perpendicular to the primary branch

Only allow two branches to originate from a single point

Remove branches returning to the center of the tree

Remove crossing branches

Developmental pruning continues to build form by removing and shaping secondary branches.

Wiring to shape

Wire is used to manipulate both the trunk and branches of bonsai to give them the form and direction needed to create your desired style. The thickening of the vascular tissues in spring and fall eventually allows the tree to hold this new shape permanently.

HOW TO WIRE A BRANCH

Wire in spring before growth or in late fall after leaf drop. Branches are wired in pairs, with the wire anchored around the trunk to hold them in place. Coil wire around each branch, keeping the twists evenly spaced, tightly fitted to the branch, and pitched at about 60°. Run multiple wires parallel where they need to run along the same length of branch. Always cut wire neatly so that it ends under the branch tip.

Avoid:

• Untidy, protruding wire ends.
• Unevenly spaced or badly angled wiring.
• Overly loose or tight wiring.
• Crossing wires.
• Using wire of the wrong thickness.
• Damage to needles, leaves, or buds.

Which wire?

Two types of wire are used to style bonsai: copper and anodized aluminum. Copper wire is more stable, but harder to work with. Its rough surface can injure thin-barked trees, so it is usually used for conifers. Aluminum wire is more flexible and easier to handle. Its smooth surface is ideal for delicate deciduous trees, such as maples. See tree profiles for advice on the correct type of wire to use. Choose a gauge of wire around one third of the diameter of the branches to be shaped.

Aluminum and copper wire

REMOVING WIRE AND PREVENTING SCARS

Always remove wire from thin-barked deciduous trees before it bites into the bark (6–12 months). Scars in the thick bark of evergreens heal over, so wire can be left to bite in (up to 2 years). Cushion wire by wrapping it in moist paper towel, to help prevent scars on thin-barked species.

WIRING TECHNIQUES AND MANIPULATION

Structural wiring shapes the trunk and primary branches and is crucial for establishing the form of any bonsai. The thinner secondary branches should also be wired to continue to enhance the image of the tree.

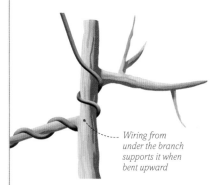

Wiring from under the branch supports it when bent upward

Bring wire onto the branch from above to bend downward

1 Use a single length of wire to style a pair of primary branches and anchor it around the trunk. Starting from the trunk, twist the wire up from below the branch if you wish to bend it upwards. This supports the branch and helps prevent it snapping.

2 To bend a branch downward, twist the wire down from above the point where the trunk meets the branch. Finish by coiling the wire evenly around both branches, right from the base to the tip.

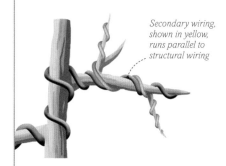

Secondary wiring, shown in yellow, runs parallel to structural wiring

Support the branch near the trunk with one hand while bending

3 Wire secondary branches at the same time as primary branches. Anchor a thinner piece of wire around the primary branch and twist it parallel to the thicker structural wire, before coiling it along each secondary branch. Don't cross the wires.

4 Bend wired branches carefully to follow the theme of the defining branch (see p.33), or style them as you choose. Giving branches similar lines creates a consistent, and usually more beautiful, bonsai.

Starting a young tree

Nurturing a young tree involves patience and many important decisions, but gives you the freedom to create a bonsai that is entirely your own. Choose a tree species that is native to your location to make cultivation straightforward.

INITIAL DEVELOPMENT

Allow a young tree to grow freely at this stage, building up foliage and energy. Feed and water it regularly to bulk up the trunk and branches. Once the tree is established and strong, prune and wire to select and begin shaping the "defining branch" and primary branches (see pp.32–33). "Sacrificial branches," not needed in the final design, can be kept to help thicken a certain area of the tree (usually the trunk below the branch) and create a tapered trunk. They are removed once this growth has occurred.

Allow the tree to grow freely before pruning

A large sacrificial branch helps boost growth

It is important to thicken the trunk at this stage

Ideally, plant a young tree in the soil outdoors

Initial development is a phase lasting from 2–6 years, during which a young tree is planted in the soil or a large pot.

LATER DEVELOPMENT

Transfer the tree into a container that is much larger and deeper than the final bonsai pot. The goal is now to establish the final structure of the tree (see p.32–33). Do this by pruning back the primary branches to produce thinner secondary branches, along with back buds away from the branch tips (see pp.34–35). Remove any sacrificial branches. Use wire (see p.36–37) to finalize the form of primary branches and give secondary branches their initial shape. Continue to feed and water the tree generously, to keep it growing strongly in its pot.

STARTING TO REFINE

Refinement can begin once the structure of the primary and secondary branches has taken shape. Pinching out the shoot tips of some species in early spring redirects energy to existing back buds (see p.49), and selective pruning of areas producing strong growth helps promote balance and stimulate weaker parts of the tree. As the back buds develop, the tree becomes denser and produces smaller foliage. Moderate the supply of water and fertilizer now to prevent branches thickening excessively, allowing them to taper and form finer branching at the tips.

Remove the strong leading shoot to create a new apex

Prune out any poorly placed branches

Take off the sacrificial branch

Pinch out tips of shoots in early spring

The defining branch is taking shape

Choose a bonsai pot for your tree

Development shapes a tree for the next 2–5 years, when it is grown on in a ceramic training pot or wooden box.

Refinement enhances the tree's form and takes between 2 and 5 years. Only now can a tree be planted in its final bonsai pot.

Make a cascade

The dramatic cascade form demonstrates the struggle between a powerful old tree and the forces of nature in high alpine regions. Conifers suit this bonsai style, because they can be found in mountain habitats, with their growth forced downward by strong winds.

CREATING A STRONG CASCADE

Finding a tree that already has some of the characteristics of a cascade and naturally lends itself to this style makes it easier to achieve a pleasing result. Bonsai is all about "listening to the tree," rather than using techniques to mold it into something that it is not meant to be.

Angle of the trunk

A good cascade has a trunk that is bent or angled, at or near its base, to grow roughly horizontally or even downward. This can be created by wiring a young tree, but strong bends must be wired for a long time, which often causes scars. It is better to find a tree that already has this feature.

Anchor roots

These surface roots reach in the opposite direction to the trunk. They are usually quite subtle, so as not to compete with the trunk's movement, but junipers often have prominent, curling anchor roots. Roots can be grafted where none are present, but choosing a young tree with roots in the desired position is much simpler.

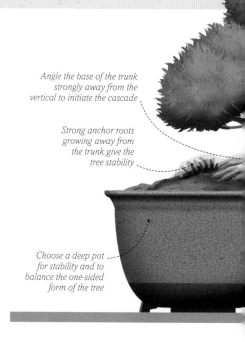

Angle the base of the trunk strongly away from the vertical to initiate the cascade

Strong anchor roots growing away from the trunk give the tree stability

Choose a deep pot for stability and to balance the one-sided form of the tree

Cascading bonsai are placed in a raised position on a table or stand to allow their branches to fall below the base of the pot.

Branches on the upper part of the trunk are directed upward to counter the strong cascading movement

SHAPING BRANCHES

Branches will need to be wired to create a cascade. When positioning branches, keep in mind the tree trying to grow upward despite the natural elements forcing it downward.

1 Wire the main and secondary branches in pairs (see p.37) to enable them to be shaped. To manipulate a branch, use one hand to hold it at its junction with the trunk, where the most force is exerted, and the other hand to bend it downward.

2 To create a natural shape, ensure that the branch is bent slightly toward the "front" of the tree, which is the side from which the bonsai is viewed. Branch tips bearing foliage should also be directed upward gently, to mimic growth toward sunlight.

Initially, cascading branches move downward, but their tips grow up toward the light

Make a rock planting

Rock plantings allow the creation of spectacular landscapes with only a few small trees, which are usually conifers. The rock is fully incorporated into the design, and often acts as a trunk, carrying bonsai that represent the foliage of the tree.

FINDING HARMONY IN TREE AND ROCK

When all the key features of a rock planting are considered, a harmonious composition of trees and stone can be achieved.

• The rock is the foundation of the design and needs to have the correct proportions to carry the trees, as well as a natural, aged, mountain character with no tool marks.

• Choose tree species that would grow on the type of rock selected in their native habitat.

• Compose an image combining both foliage form and negative space, to help highlight the texture and features of the stone.

• In nature, the highest tree would be the most exposed to harsh weather and its character sets the tone for the trees below.

GUIDING ROOTS IN MOSS VEINS

Allowing tree roots to access a pot of soil at the base of a rock planting makes watering and repotting easier. When planting, wrap roots in wet moss and push them into crevices filled with keto clay and a mix of akadama and moss. These paths provide roots with a way to grow down into the pot.

Conifers are usually used in rock plantings and each should be a characterful, carefully shaped bonsai

Covering the soil surface with moss softens the base of the rock and creates a natural appearance

Roots from all trees on the rock can grow down into the pot to access water and nutrients

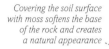

Rock plantings use cascading trees on high ledges and upright trees lower down to represent the effects of wind and snow on their growth.

The rock has a natural, textured appearance, a dark color, and offers several locations to position trees

ANCHORING TECHNIQUES

Once positions for your trees have been decided, add wires to fix them in place. Prune and shape trees before planting.

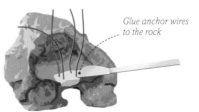

Glue anchor wires to the rock

1 Hook anchor wires in crevices or drilled holes. Secure the wires to the rock using a suitable two-component glue, following the manufacturer's instructions.

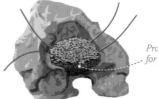

Provide soil for planting

2 Make a bed of moss or create a nook for planting from keto clay. Add a layer of a suitable akadama soil mix for the tree species, to create a foundation for the roots.

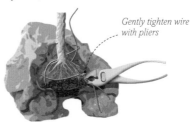

Gently tighten wire with pliers

3 Position the tree and wrap the anchor wires over the roots. Twist the wire ends with pliers to secure. Cover roots with soil and finish with a layer of moss.

Make a root-over-rock

This fascinating style displays the ability of roots to cling to a rock above soil level while still supporting the trunk. Any species with strong root growth can be grown in this way, which includes most deciduous trees and many conifers.

CHARACTERISTICS OF ROOT-OVER-ROCK

The goal of this planting style is to imbue the tree with a sense of age and suggest its struggle for survival in tough conditions. It is important to find harmony between the tree and the rock, while allowing the powerful grip of the roots to dominate the strength of the stone.

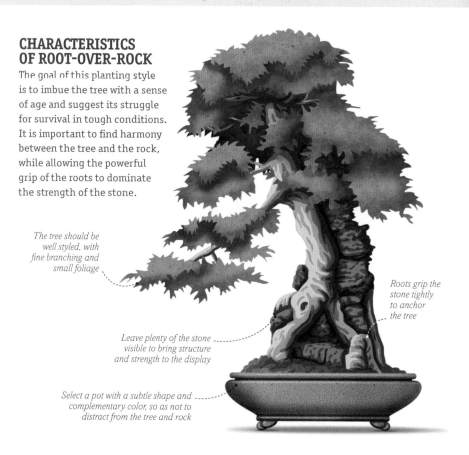

The tree should be well styled, with fine branching and small foliage

Roots grip the stone tightly to anchor the tree

Leave plenty of the stone visible to bring structure and strength to the display

Select a pot with a subtle shape and complementary color, so as not to distract from the tree and rock

REPOTTING AND WRAPPING OF ROOTS

To create a naturalistic display, the tree and rock must both be carefully positioned, secured, and repotted to develop together underground. Roots grow and thicken best beneath the soil and can be revealed once they have knitted to the rock.

Cut paste helps prevent disease after pruning

1 Prune the branches back hard and seal each wound with cut paste. This creates the initial structure of the tree and is the first stage in bonsai development.

2 Remove the tree from its pot and untangle the roots. Cut off damaged roots cleanly with sharp scissors. Select a rock that suits the shape of the roots, and position the roots over it.

3 Wrap the roots tightly against the rock with plastic tape, to guide their growth in the desired direction. Leave long roots free at the base to grow into the pot.

New growth is a sign of healthy roots

4 Plant the rock and roots into a deep pot and fill with sharp sand to the base of the trunk. A period underground enables the roots to grow strongly and thicken.

5 Keep the tree in the pot for at least one year, while the roots develop and cling tightly to the rock. New shoots will also form during this time. Water the tree regularly during growth.

6 Once the roots have knitted into the textured surface of the rock, remove the plastic tape and plant in a bonsai pot, using the soil mix listed for the tree profile.

Creating *jin* and *shari*

Deadwood on bonsai signifies age and its sculptural qualities bring character to a tree. Unlike living wood, it has no covering of bark, which can create dramatic color contrasts on a trunk. Natural, aged deadwood is highly valued and many techniques exist to imitate it.

DEADWOOD ON LIVING TREES

Deadwood is most often seen on conifer bonsai, because they are able to compartmentalize dead and living tissue and their resinous sap acts as a preservative. Pines form smooth, cylindrical deadwood, and junipers create blade-like, dramatically lined features. A few deciduous trees, such as *Prunus* species, also produce attractive and long-lasting deadwood.

CONSERVING DEADWOOD

Deadwood needs to be conserved as it ages to prevent rotting. In alpine habitats, wind and sunlight inhibit rotting and "sandblast" deadwood, turning it white over time. In bonsai, this natural process is emulated as follows:
• Clean deadwood annually, using water and a soft plastic brush to remove dirt and algae.
• Use lime sulfur annually, to bleach and preserve deadwood that has dried and aged for at least one year. Clean and wet the area with a soft plastic brush. Wear eye protection, gloves, and cover surfaces. Apply lime sulfur carefully with a brush.

Pale deadwood *jin* and *shari* create striking swirling forms among the foliage of this Chinese juniper.

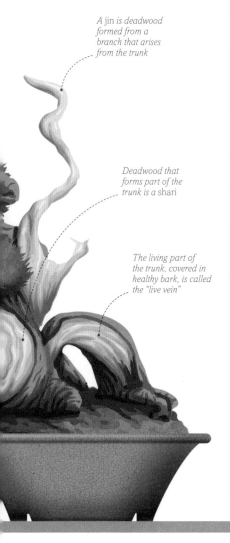

A jin *is deadwood formed from a branch that arises from the trunk*

Deadwood that forms part of the trunk is a shari

The living part of the trunk, covered in healthy bark, is called the "live vein"

REMOVING BARK AND SHAPING DEADWOOD

Creating deadwood adds character to a young bonsai. Use the pruned stub of a branch to form a naturalistic feature.

1 To create a *jin*, score around the base of a branch stub with concave cutters. Crush bark with jinning pliers to loosen it and pull it away to expose pale wood.

2 Shape the *jin* by peeling back wood fibers with jinning pliers. This gradually refines the shape and adds texture. Extend the tear into the trunk to create a *shari*.

3 Once shaped, use a wire brush to clean and smooth the wood's surface, while retaining its naturalistic appearance. Don't apply lime sulfur until wood has aged.

Maintenance pruning

Routine pruning of branches and roots is vital to maintain the structure and carefully crafted image of your bonsai. Pruning of the branches is typically carried out once or twice a year, while work on the root structure is often done during repotting.

ROOT PRUNING

Roots are pruned each time a tree is repotted. Remove any larger anchoring roots to encourage the development of fine feeding roots, which take up nutrients and water, and are much more useful to a tree growing in a small pot. Remove a maximum of 30 percent of the living root mass. To refine the *nebari* (root flare), shorten any crossing or long, protruding roots to form an even, radial pattern of surface roots.

Prune roots using bonsai scissors

Hinoki cypress (pp.68–69)

TRIMMING

This technique is used in the refinement of a tree, once the branch structure is established. New growth is trimmed to maintain its form and increase ramification (the structure of fine branches). Use sharp scissors or concave cutters to trim back shoots to two buds, so that two new, finer shoots will form, creating a bifurcation. All tree species should be trimmed, usually from early to midsummer.

Cut vigorous new growth to retain your tree's shape

Japanese quince (pp.66–67)

DEFOLIATING

Removing healthy leaves from trees is a refinement technique and should only be carried out on mature trees that have developed their final form. Defoliation is used to allow light to reach inner buds, preventing them from dying off and increasing the tree's potential for further ramification. The leaves produced following defoliation are also smaller, which suits the compact form of bonsai trees well. Partial defoliation (removal of up to half the foliage) can be performed on most deciduous trees, and is usually carried out in early summer. Reserve full defoliation for healthy specimens of the strongest-growing species, which include trident and Japanese maples.

Cut leaf stalks cleanly with sharp scissors

Japanese maple (pp.58–59)

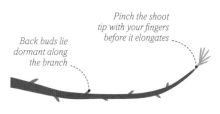

Pinch the shoot tip with your fingers before it elongates

Back buds lie dormant along the branch

New growth at the shoot tip

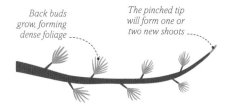

Back buds grow, forming dense foliage

The pinched tip will form one or two new shoots

Pinching stimulates bushy growth

PINCHING

Pinching out the shoot tips as they start growing prevents shoots elongating and allows back buds away from the tip of the branch to develop instead (secondary growth). This gives the tree a fuller, bushier, more mature appearance, and keeps its form compact and attractive. Pinching should only be carried out during the refinement phase of a tree's development, once the structure of main branches has been established. It is best done by hand, between early and late spring, depending on the species. This technique works well for most conifers and deciduous trees, but check tree profiles for the few species that do not respond well to pinching.

Pests and diseases

When cared for correctly, bonsai are not generally prone to problems, but common insect pests and unsuitable growing conditions can lead to a deterioration in both the appearance and health of your trees.

CREATING STRONG DEFENSES

Regular watering allows every part of the tree to function correctly, and is vital for trees kept in shallow bonsai pots. Healthy. trees are equipped with defensive agents to protect against pests and diseases. Some of these are produced by microorganisms in the soil, which can be encouraged by feeding with an organic fertilizer.

COMMON PROBLEMS

Aphids

Small, sap-sucking insects including greenfly, which vary in color, size, and shape. They cause tiny pale spots and yellowing on young foliage. Remove by hand or with water and a little soap.

Aphids multiply rapidly beneath young leaves

An aphid colony

Spider mites

In ideal warm, dry conditions, these microscopic mites can quickly infest a whole tree, causing an overall weakening and graying of foliage, which may eventually die. Wash off thoroughly with water and try increasing humidity.

Fine, silky webbing betrays spider mites

Spider mite infestation

"**Healthy trees** are equipped with **their own defensive agents** against pests and diseases."

Caterpillars

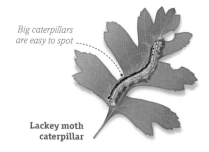

Sometimes well camouflaged, the holes and deformities these larvae cause on foliage are usually what gives them away. Pick off by hand or wash off using water and a little dish soap.

Big caterpillars are easy to spot

Lackey moth caterpillar

Mildew

White fungal growth coats leaves, blocking light, and weakening the tree. This can arise if foliage remains wet or plants are under watered. Improve growing conditions or treat with an appropriate fungicide.

White patches mark the upper leaf surface

Mildew symptoms on an oak leaf

Root rot

This fungal disease causes roots to turn brown and die. New shoots also weaken, yellow, and die back. Often caused by soil waterlogging, so repot into a fresh, aerated soil mix. A suitable fungicide can also help.

OTHER PROBLEMS

Learn to recognize the symptoms of these pests and diseases and monitor your trees regularly for any signs of trouble. Treated promptly, most problems can be resolved without causing any lasting damage.

• **Root aphids** are small, white insects that suck sap from roots. They are usually only noticed during repotting and can be hard to remove. Feed and water regularly to maximize the tree's health and treat with a systemic insecticide.

• **Scale insects and mealybugs** are small sap-sucking insects, which hide in crevices and along stems, and multiply rapidly. Scale insects have a hard, yellow-brown shell, while mealy bugs are covered in waxy, white hairs. Pick or wash off small numbers by hand. Use a systemic insecticide for severe infestations.

• **Verticillium wilt** is a fungal disease which affects the vascular tissue within the branches, causing new shoots to wilt and branches to die back. No chemical treatment is available.

• **Rust** produces small, raised orange or yellow spots, surrounded by discoloration, on leaves. It is a fungal disease, which left untreated can cause foliage to die off. Remove affected leaves promptly and treat with a systemic fungicide.

• **Leaf spot diseases** can be caused by fungi or bacteria and result in brown, circular marks on foliage and sometimes leaf drop. Although unsightly, they do not usually affect the tree significantly. Remove affected leaves. Fungal cases can be treated with a systemic fungicide.

BONSAI **PROFILES**

Trident maple

Acer buergerianum

This vigorous Asian maple makes an ideal deciduous bonsai, thanks to its ability to heal pruning wounds, and to form a dense structure of fine branches and a good *nebari* (root-flare). Shiny, trident-shaped leaves turn fiery orange and red in fall, and its smooth bark develops platelike texture with age.

WATER
Keep soil evenly moist by watering up to twice daily during summer and less often in winter. Monitor trees in shallow pots carefully, because maples can lose their leaves if kept too dry. This species will tolerate hard tap water.

Origin
Native to East Asia, where these trees can reach up to 66 ft (20 m) in height.

How it grows
A deciduous tree with new leaves produced in pairs, beautiful fall color, and flaky bark on mature specimens.

Position
Grow outdoors in full sun or semi-shade. It is less vulnerable to fungal diseases in a sunny and more exposed spot.

Special care
More tolerant of full sun than other maples, but move tree to semi-shade in hot, dry weather, to prevent leaf scorch.

WIRE
Wire bare branches in fall, in spring before new growth, or after any defoliation. Use aluminum wire and be careful with the brittle branches. Wrap wire in wet cloth and remove it in good time to prevent scarring.

FEED

Apply a nitrogen-rich organic fertilizer once a month throughout the growing season, then switch to a potassium- and phosphate-rich fall feed to produce more intense fall color.

PRUNE

This vigorous species can be pruned throughout the growing season from late spring until late summer. Defoliate dense trees, fully or partially, during summer. This allows in light to keep inner buds alive. Suits all styles; try *moyogi* (informal upright).

An informal upright grown root-over-rock

REPOT

Repot every 3–5 years in spring before buds burst. Prune roots at the same time to create a strong *nebari* (root-flare). Use a soil mix of equal parts akadama and lava or pumice.

Amur maple

Acer ginnala

Also known as the fire maple, this vigorous tree is the first maple to show its vibrant fall color as the days grow shorter. Its three-lobed leaves are similar to those of the trident maple, but with less prominent side lobes. Mature trees develop characterful bark and *nebari* (root-flare), and also produce small, white flowers, followed by red fruits during summer.

WATER

Water up to twice daily in summer and less often during winter to keep soil consistently moist. Maples can drop their leaves if kept too dry, so monitor the soil moisture, particularly when grown in a shallow pot. This species tolerates hard tap water.

Origin
Native to the Balkans and northern steppes bordering the Black Sea, where it reaches 33 ft (10 m) tall.

How it grows
A deciduous tree, early into spring growth. The foliage colors well in fall and mature trees develop flaky bark.

Position
Give it full sun or semi-shade outdoors. Tolerant of high summer temperatures, it is also frost- and wind-hardy.

Special care
The young foliage needs protection against late frosts. Protect roots, too, in areas with cold winter weather.

WIRE

Maples are brittle, so use only aluminum wire to bend their bare branches in fall, in spring before new growth, or after a defoliation. Avoid scars by wrapping wire in a wet cloth before applying, and removing in good time.

FEED

Use an organic nitrogen-rich feed once a month during growth, changing to a potassium- and phosphate-rich feed in fall for more intense fall color.

REPOT

Repot every 3–5 years in spring before growth begins. Encourage the production of a strong *nebari* (root-flare) by root pruning every time you repot. Use a moisture-retentive, free-draining mix, containing akadama and lava or pumice in equal ratios.

Come fall the leaves turn vivid yellow, orange, and red

Pruned in the rounded broom style, this tree has an upright trunk

PRUNE

Can be pruned throughout the growing season, from late spring until late summer. Wounds are slow to callus (heal) on this species, so only remove one branch at a time where necessary. Full or partial defoliation in summer allows light to reach inner buds on dense trees. Suits upright styles; try *moyogi* (informal upright).

Japanese maple

Acer palmatum

Cultivated as bonsai in Japan for centuries, this maple has year-round appeal. Smooth bark and fine branches create winter form, while the fan-shaped leaves turn from fresh spring hues to dramatic red in fall. Attractive cultivars, such as 'Seigen' and 'Deshojo', are more sensitive than the species.

WATER

Maples can drop their leaves if kept too dry, so monitor trees in shallow bonsai pots carefully. Water up to twice daily during summer and less in winter to keep soil moist. Use rainwater, because they are sensitive to hard water.

WIRE

Wire brittle maple branches when they are bare in fall, before new spring growth, or after partial defoliation. Use aluminum wire. Wrap wire in a wet cloth before applying and remove it in good time to avoid scars.

 Origin
Native to Japan, Korea, China, eastern Mongolia, and Russia, where it can reach 33 ft (10 m) high.

 How it grows
A deciduous, upright tree, with fine foliage, beautiful fall color, and gray, fissured bark on mature trees.

 Position
Give it a semi-shaded spot, especially when grown in a shallow bonsai pot. Leaves scorch easily in heat and full sun.

 Special care
Provide root protection in winter and lower soil pH by adding *Kanuma* (azalea soil), or ericaceous compost.

REPOT

Repot every 3–5 years in spring before growth. Use a mix of akadama and lava or pumice in equal ratios. Prune roots to promote a good *nebari* (root-flare).

FEED

Apply an organic, high-nitrogen feed monthly during growth, but switch to a potassium- and phosphate-rich feed in fall to intensify fall color and prevent soft growth before winter.

PRUNE

Prune only after new leaves are fully developed and "hardened off" (toughened and darker colored) in early summer; before this the tree will bleed sap. Pinch to control new growth. Partially defoliate dense trees to keep inner buds alive. Suits upright styles; try *yose-ue* (forest).

Cultivar 'Deshojo' makes a striking informal upright

Bougainvillea

Bougainvillea

The vibrant flowers of Bougainvillea are actually a type of colorful leaf, surrounding the pale true flower at their center. A subtropical shrub, it grows strongly outdoors in warm climates, and will also thrive when cultivated carefully as an indoor bonsai during winter in cooler regions, where temperatures fall below 41°F (5°C).

WATER

Water daily during summer and less frequently during winter to keep the soil evenly moist. Always allow the soil surface to dry before you water again.

FEED

Apply an organic balanced fertilizer monthly once flowering has finished, usually in midsummer, until fall. This will guarantee a great start to the following season.

Origin
Native to much of South America, where these tall shrubs can reach up to 16 ft (5 m) in height.

 How it grows
A vigorous evergreen with a bushy habit, ideal for creating dense bonsai. Watch out for the thorny stems.

Position
Give it a sunny, sheltered outdoor position during growth and a bright spot indoors in winter with a minimum of 41°F (5°C).

Special care
When moving back outdoors in spring, first place the plant in shade, and gradually move into full sun to prevent scorch.

PRUNE

Prune in midsummer, after flowering and when feeding begins. New growth appears in 3–4 weeks, which can then be pruned again. Stop pruning at the end of the growing season, about a month before moving to its winter home. Try *moyogi* (informal upright) or *kengai* (cascade) style.

A twisted trunk may be natural or sculpted when a plant is young

The 'Blondie' cultivar has vivid pink blooms and suits cascade style

WIRE

Bougainvilleas are very brittle, but branches can be wired and moved into position carefully throughout the year using aluminum wire.

REPOT

Repot before moving outdoors, every 3–5 years. Add a drainage layer of bigger lava or pumice, and plant into a mix of akadama and lava or pumice, in equal ratios.

European hornbeam

Carpinus betulus

This vigorous tree has many qualities well-suited to bonsai, such as smooth, gray bark, fine branches, elegant small buds, and an increasingly characterful trunk. Mature trees can develop attractive texture and deadwood on their trunks and old *yamadori* (wild-collected trees) can become great fairy-tale-style bonsai.

WATER

Water daily in summer to keep the soil evenly moist, as hornbeams tend to lose their leaves if kept too dry. Reduce watering during winter. They are sensitive to hard water, so use rainwater if possible.

A semi-cascade style with twin trunks looks elegant year-round

 Origin
Native to forests in southern Europe, where these trees can reach a height of up to 82 ft (25 m).

 How it grows
This deciduous tree has pointed, alternate leaves that may turn rich yellow in fall, and develops fine, gray bark.

 Position
Give it a bright position outdoors, out of direct sunlight, especially when cultivated in a small bonsai pot.

 Special care
Grown as a bonsai, the leaves scorch easily in full sun, especially above 86°F (30°C), so grow in semi-shade or full shade.

WIRE

Wire when the branch structure is visible in fall after leaf drop, in spring before new growth, or after partial defoliation. Use only aluminum wire on the brittle branches. Avoid wire scars by wrapping the wire in a wet cloth before applying and removing the wire in good time.

FEED

Fertilize monthly with a balanced organic feed through spring and summer. Switch to feed high in phosphorous and potassium in fall to prevent excessive soft growth before winter.

PRUNE

Prune once new leaves are hardened off in early summer. Pinch to control vigor in the early stages of development. Partially defoliate dense trees to keep inner buds alive and reduce leaf size. Callus formation (wound healing) is good when enough branches are left around the cut. Suits *han-kengai* (semi-cascade) and all upright styles.

REPOT

Repot every 3–5 years, before growth in spring. Prune roots to form a strong *nebari* (root-flare). Use a moisture-retentive 1:1 mix of lava or pumice and akadama.

Australian pine

Casuarina equisetifolia

The combination of the soft needle pads of classical pine bonsai, with spotted, light gray bark, gives this evergreen conifer its own unique style. It can produce an attractive *nebari* (root-flare) and quickly grow into a beautiful form, resembling the traditional Japanese white pine. Its subtropical origins make it a perfect indoor bonsai.

WATER

This species is very drought-tolerant, so although it will need regular watering in summer, always allow the soil surface to dry out before watering.

WIRE

Younger shoots are quite flexible and can be positioned using aluminum or copper wire. Wire in fall or in spring before new growth. Remove wire before it digs into the bark.

Origin
Native to tropical and subtropical Australia, where trees can reach up to 115 ft (35 m) high.

How it grows
The thin leaves of this evergreen tree resemble pine needles. Mature trees develop spotted gray bark.

Position
Give it full sun outdoors for the growing season. Keep indoors in a bright spot for winter, with a minimum of 41°F (5°C).

Special care
Gradually acclimate this robust tropical species to direct sunlight when it is moved outdoors in spring.

Pruning and pinching will create dense pads of needles

FEED

Fertilize monthly with a balanced organic fertilizer during growth. Stop feeding toward the end of the growing season and do not feed while indoors for winter.

REPOT

Repot every 3–5 years, in spring before new growth. Use a well-aerated soil mix to provide good drainage, combining akadama, lava, and pumice in equal ratios.

PRUNE

Prune after new leaves are fully developed (3 in/8 cm long) in late spring. Cut new growth back to 1 in (2 cm) long. Pinch to create dense needle pads when there are enough back buds (buds away from the shoot tip). Suits *han-kengai* (semi-cascade) and *moyogi* (informal upright) styles.

Wide roots and a tapered trunk add balance to this semi-cascade specimen

Japanese quince

Chaenomeles japonica

With its vivid red flowers borne on bare stems from late winter to early spring, this is a true beauty and a gem among bonsai species. It is highly regarded for its ability to form tiny leaves and a structure of fine branches, known as "ramification," but beware of the needle-sharp thorns.

WATER
Keep soil consistently moist by watering shallow pots twice a day in hot summer weather, less frequently in cooler conditions. Use rainwater or soft tap water.

Long-lasting flowers open from colorful, spherical buds

 Origin
Native to Japan and China, and widely grown as a garden shrub, it can reach 3 ft (1 m) high or more.

 How it grows
A winter-flowering deciduous shrub, with small, glossy, green leaves and even growth that is easily molded.

WIRE
Wiring is rarely needed as this species branches strongly, but aluminum wire can be used in spring before new growth or in fall. Remove wire before it bites into bark.

 **Position**
Prefers a bright position in full sun, but will also tolerate semi-shade.

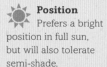 **Special care**
Fine new shoots formed after pruning need protection from winter frosts, under cover in a cool, bright place.

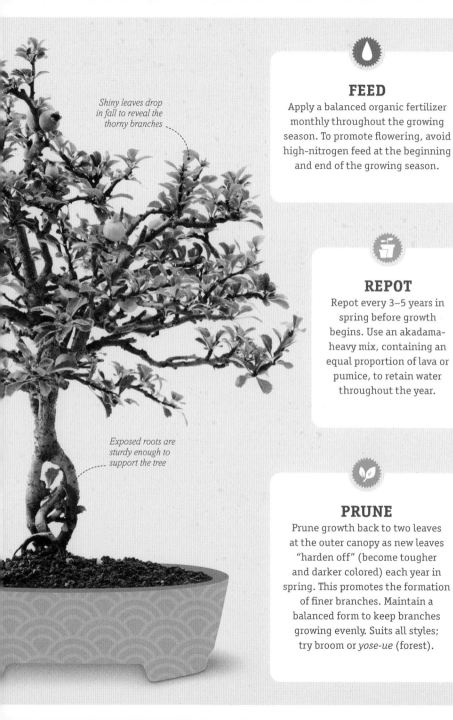

Shiny leaves drop in fall to reveal the thorny branches

Exposed roots are sturdy enough to support the tree

FEED

Apply a balanced organic fertilizer monthly throughout the growing season. To promote flowering, avoid high-nitrogen feed at the beginning and end of the growing season.

REPOT

Repot every 3–5 years in spring before growth begins. Use an akadama-heavy mix, containing an equal proportion of lava or pumice, to retain water throughout the year.

PRUNE

Prune growth back to two leaves at the outer canopy as new leaves "harden off" (become tougher and darker colored) each year in spring. This promotes the formation of finer branches. Maintain a balanced form to keep branches growing evenly. Suits all styles; try broom or *yose-ue* (forest).

Hinoki cypress

Chamaecyparis obtusa

WATER

Use rainwater to keep the soil consistently moist. Shallow bonsai pots may need watering twice a day in summer, but less frequently during cooler weather. Increase humidity by misting the foliage regularly in summer.

This is an outstanding conifer for bonsai and there are many famous examples of Hinoki bonsai in Japan. Its dark brown, fissured bark contrasts with soft pads of evergreen foliage to great effect year-round. The naturally powerful growth suits the upright style as a solitary tree, in a group, or as a twin-trunk.

Tiny, scale-like leaves form a dense canopy

🌍 Origin
Native to East Asia, especially southern Japan, where trees reach up to 140 ft (40 m) tall.

🌱 How it grows
An evergreen, upright tree, usually with a straight trunk and branches bearing fans of scale-like foliage.

☀ Position
Give it full sun or semi-shade outdoors. Provide winter protection in a greenhouse or a cool, bright place indoors.

➕ Special care
Clean off older foliage scales when they turn brown. Move into partial shade and mist regularly in summer.

WIRE

Wire in fall or in spring before new growth appears. Use a thick gauge of copper wire to move the main branches and a finer gauge for thinner secondary branches. Avoid wire scars by removing the wire in good time.

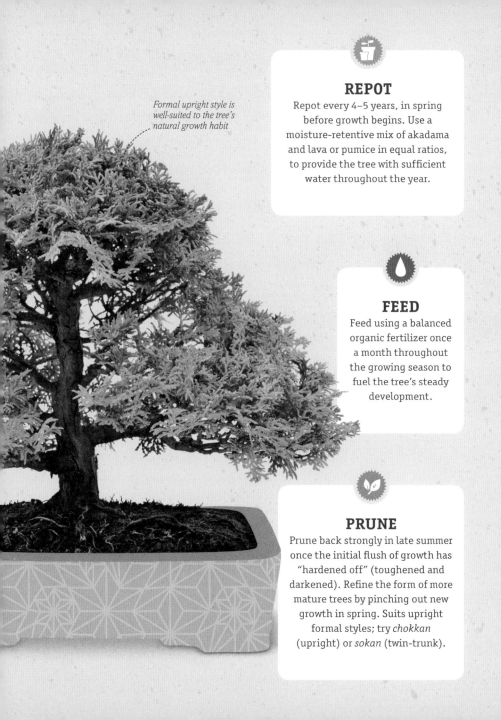

Formal upright style is well-suited to the tree's natural growth habit

REPOT

Repot every 4–5 years, in spring before growth begins. Use a moisture-retentive mix of akadama and lava or pumice in equal ratios, to provide the tree with sufficient water throughout the year.

FEED

Feed using a balanced organic fertilizer once a month throughout the growing season to fuel the tree's steady development.

PRUNE

Prune back strongly in late summer once the initial flush of growth has "hardened off" (toughened and darkened). Refine the form of more mature trees by pinching out new growth in spring. Suits upright formal styles; try *chokkan* (upright) or *sokan* (twin-trunk).

Tokonoma display

A *tokonoma* is an alcove inside a traditional Japanese house, where decorative objects are displayed to honor a guest or mark the passing seasons. Large bonsai are often central to compositions in these generous, framed spaces. Traditional tokonoma displays produce harmony between a single tree on a table, a background scroll, and a small accent plant. Every detail, down to the pattern on the pot, is imbued with significance and meaning.

These temporary indoor displays are usually kept in place for around a week, before the tree is returned to its position outdoors. Tokonoma displays can often be seen at bonsai exhibitions. In the West, bonsai enthusiasts also make use of outdoor alcoves to present tokonoma-inspired displays.

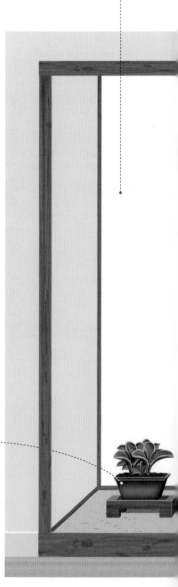

A tokonoma provides a pale, framed canvas for display, accentuating light and shadow

The accent plant may represent the season or simply contrast the tree in form, texture, or leaf size

A background scroll *(kakejiku)* suggests a landscape or season without being too explicit

KEEP IT SIMPLE
Present your bonsai on a sideboard in a bright spot, with a small houseplant as an accent plant, and a framed picture in place of a scroll.

A large, mature bonsai at least 2 ft (60 cm) tall is needed, with a traditional moss covering on the soil

Direct the flow of the bonsai branches toward the accent plant

The table or stand should fit the character of the tree but not outshine it

Cotoneaster

Cotoneaster horizontalis

The miniature proportions of the dark green leaves; five-petaled, white flowers; and spherical red fruits make this species perfect for bonsai cultivation. It is the ideal candidate for even the smallest bonsai styles. The foliage also turns intense shades of red and orange before dropping in fall.

WATER

Water regularly to keep soil consistently moist throughout the year, particularly when plants are flowering and fruiting. When kept in a shallow bonsai pot it may be necessary to water twice day during hot summer weather.

WIRE

Use aluminum wire to bend bare shoots in fall or in spring before new growth appears. Flexible younger branches can be positioned easily. Avoid scars by removing wire before it bites into the wood.

 Origin
Native to Europe, North Africa, and Asia, this dense shrub can reach 3 ft (1 m) tall.

 How it grows
A spreading, deciduous shrub, it grows evenly, producing shoots in all directions, making it easy to shape.

 Position
Give it full sun or semi-shade outdoors. Move under cover for winter to avoid frost damage to branch tips.

 Special care
The ripe red fruits are tempting to hungry birds: protect the display where necessary.

FEED

Apply a balanced organic fertilizer once a month from the end of flowering until the growing season comes to a close.

REPOT

Repot every 3–5 years, in spring, before growth begins. Use a moisture-retentive mix of akadama with an equal proportion of lava or pumice, to provide good drainage.

White flowers in spring precede the red berries

Deadwood counterbalances the cascade style to spectacular effect

PRUNE

Pruning to create a good structure is important to keep the branches growing evenly. Prune in spring when new leaves have "hardened off" (toughened and darkened). Leave two buds on each shoot to encourage finer branches to form. Suits all styles; try *moyogi* (informal upright) or *kengai* (cascade).

English hawthorn

Crataegus monogyna

This tough, thorny, deciduous tree boasts many attractive characteristics that suit bonsai well. Its small, serrated leaves, late spring clusters of soft white flowers, red fruits, and bright yellow fall color mean that it looks spectacular throughout the seasons. It also has finely fissured bark, and is suitable for incorporating deadwood features.

WATER
Monitor the soil daily and keep it consistently moist. Shallow bonsai pots may need watering twice a day in hot summer weather and less frequently in cooler seasons.

WIRE
Wire young shoots, using aluminum wire, and bend to shape in fall or in spring before new growth. Older branches are stiff and break easily. Avoid wire scars by removing wire in good time.

Origin
Native to the temperate northern hemisphere, where trees reach up to 30 ft (10 m) high.

How it grows
A deciduous tree, on which a few branches can dominate. Buds on the trunk can be spurred into growth by pruning.

Position
Give it a bright, sunny, well-ventilated position. Although it is hardy, protect from long periods of winter frost.

Special care
Take care when handling, because the branches are armed with strong thorns. Cut off the thorns to avoid injuries.

*Red berries
follow dainty
spring flowers*

FEED

Apply a balanced fertilizer throughout
the growing season. Avoid using high-
nitrogen feeds at the beginning and end
of the growing season to encourage
flowers and fruits to form.

REPOT

Repot before spring growth,
every 3–5 years. Use a
heavy mix of akadama and lava
or pumice in equal ratios, which
will retain sufficient water
throughout the year.

*Upright trees rise
from a fallen trunk
in this raft display*

PRUNE

Prune to create a balanced
branch structure. In spring,
once the new leaves have
"hardened off" (toughened
and darkened), cut back to two
buds at the outer canopy to
produce finer branches.
Wounds do not callus (heal
over) well, so try turning
stumps into deadwood. Suits
all styles; try fairy tale or raft.

Korean beech

Fagus crenata

A ghostly, light gray trunk; pointed, dark buds; and a dense structure of fine branches make this species an arresting sight in winter. Unusually it doesn't drop its foliage in fall, so the dry leaves are often removed by hand. Japanese nurseries supply specimens with good *nebari* (root-flare) and few scars on the trunk, allowing the bark to shine.

WATER
Keep the soil moist throughout the year. Pay close attention to watering, particularly when the tree is growing in a shallow bonsai pot, which may need watering twice a day in hot summer weather to prevent it drying out.

 Origin
Native to the forests of Japan, these trees can reach up to 100 ft (30 m) tall.

 How it grows
A deciduous tree, that retains its bronze fall foliage until spring. New shoots carry alternate leaves.

 Position
It will thrive in a bright, sunny spot outdoors, but move into semi-shade during hot summer weather.

 Special care
Although this species is hardy, give it protection from hard frosts when grown in a bonsai pot.

WIRE
Use aluminum wire to shape the young branches in fall after leaf drop or in spring before new growth appears. Avoid wire scars by removing the wire before it bites into the wood.

Bright green leaves form a rounded canopy in summer

FEED

Use a balanced organic fertilizer once a month throughout the entire growing season, to provide the tree with essential nutrients.

REPOT

Repot every 3–5 years, before growth in spring. Prune roots to produce a strong *nebari* (root-flare). Use a moisture-retentive 1:1 mix of akadama and lava or pumice.

A straight, tapering trunk is central to this formal upright

PRUNE

This species requires hard pruning. Cut back new shoots on outer parts of the tree to two buds in spring, once new leaves have "hardened off" (become tougher and darker colored). This allows light in to interior buds and promotes branching. Suits all styles; try *chokkan* (formal upright).

Natal fig

Ficus natalensis

This tropical tree is full of character, with aerial roots hanging from its branches; multiple pale trunks; and thick, glossy, dark green leaves. It thrives in the warm, humid conditions found in tropical forests, which means that, given the correct care, it makes an ideal indoor bonsai in temperate climates.

WATER

Check the pot daily and water regularly to ensure that the soil is kept consistently moist. Never allow the soil to dry out. Create high humidity by misting the foliage every day.

FEED

Use a balanced organic fertilizer once a month throughout the growing season to provide fuel for growth.

 Origin
Native to South Africa, where trees can reach 98 ft (30 m) high with wide canopies.

 How it grows
A vigorous, evergreen tree, which forms aerial roots and numerous thinner trunks in humid conditions.

 Position
Give it full sun or semi-shade indoors year-round in cool climates. Move outdoors for summer in warm areas.

 Special care
This tropical tree thrives in high humidity at around 68°F (20°C), so keep indoors in winter and mist regularly.

REPOT

Repot in spring, every 3–5 years, before growth begins. Use a moisture-retentive soil mix containing equal parts akadama and lava or pumice.

WIRE

Wire flexible young shoots after pruning using aluminum wire. Shoots thicken quickly, so take care to remove wire before it scars the branches.

PRUNE

Prune new shoots back hard to two leaves when they finish elongating in summer, to produce a good framework of finer branches. Pruning to form a balanced structure is essential to keep the vigor of branches even. Suits all styles; try natural or *moyogi* (informal upright).

Bonsai quickly appear aged because branches thicken rapidly

Aerial roots grow downward and strangle host plants in the wild

Lipstick fig

Ficus virens var. *glabella*

The brightly colored new leaves of this tropical tree give rise to its common name thanks to their resemblance to red lips. This vivid display is brief, but the lipstick fig also develops attractive aerial roots and light-colored bark. It is a vigorous "strangler" fig in its native habitat, outgrowing and finally killing its host tree, so it needs frequent pruning to keep it as a compact bonsai.

WATER

Check daily and do not allow the soil to dry out. Watering may be needed twice daily in hot summer weather, but less often in cooler conditions. Create humidity by misting the leaves regularly.

Shaped in informal upright style

 Origin
Native to tropical India, Southeast Asia, and northern Australia, these trees reach 105 ft (32 m) high with wide canopies.

 How it grows
A strong-growing evergreen, with glossy leaves. Its trunk and branches thicken quickly.

Position
Give it full sun or semi-shade outdoors in summer. Makes an ideal indoor bonsai in cool regions (see Special care).

Special care
This tropical tree needs winter protection. Move it indoors or into a greenhouse at about 68°F (20°C), with high humidity.

WIRE

The shoots are quite flexible when they are young and should be wired after pruning, using aluminum wire. They thicken very quickly, so be careful to remove the wire before it scars the branches.

FEED

Apply a balanced organic fertilizer once a month throughout the growing season.

REPOT

Repot in spring, every 4–5 years depending on the tree's development, before new growth begins. Use a moisture-retentive and free-draining soil mix containing akadama and lava or pumice in equal ratios.

New shoot tips are briefly bright red when young

The trunk and nebari *(root-flare) quickly develop an aged appearance*

PRUNE

This species can be pruned back hard and ramifies (forms a structure of fine branches) well. Prune new shoots back to two leaves in summer, as they finish elongating, to encourage branching. Maintain a good structure to keep the dense growth in check and ensure that branches develop evenly. Suits all styles; try natural or *moyogi* (informal upright).

Japanese holly

Ilex serrata

This tree is valued for the aged character of its trunk, its pink late spring flowers, and bright red fall berries. Both female and male trees are needed for a display of berries. Fruits can last throughout winter, when they hang bauble-like among the bare branches.

WATER

Keep the soil evenly moist, particularly when the tree is fruiting. Trees kept in shallow bonsai pots need to be watered twice a day in hot weather, but less at cooler times, so pay close attention to watering.

Dense foliage offsets a sturdy trunk in this moyogi tree

 Origin
Native to China and Japan where the small trees grow to 15 ft (4.5 m) tall.

 How it grows
A deciduous tree with attractive spring flowers, summer foliage, and fall berries that remain over winter.

 Position
Give it full sun or semi-shade outdoors. Move into a greenhouse or to a cool, bright spot indoors in winter.

 Special care
Once the berries have formed, protect them from hungry birds with netting or by moving the tree under cover.

WIRE

Wire in fall or in spring before new growth appears, using aluminum wire. Branches don't thicken rapidly, which makes them easy to bend into position, but take care to remove wire before it damages the bark.

FEED

Apply a balanced organic feed monthly during growth. Avoid nitrogen-rich feeds before flowering and at the end of the growing season.

PRUNE

Prune back new shoots to two buds in spring, as they "harden off" (toughen and become darker in color). Try and prune to downward-facing buds to counteract the tendency of shoots to grow vertically. Suits *moyogi* (informal upright) style.

Colorful berries become prominent once the leaves fall

REPOT

Repot every 3–4 years, in spring, before new growth begins. Prune roots to form a strong *nebari* (root-flare). Use an akadama-heavy soil mix, containing an equal proportion of lava or pumice.

California juniper

Juniperus californica

This tree is renowned for bonsai with tough, twisted deadwood and slender live veins (portions of living bark feeding the branches). The coarse, evergreen foliage is adapted to cope with the heat and drought of its native California, but given less extreme conditions it can become quite dense.

WATER
Despite its resistance to drought, water this species regularly to keep it healthy and encourage good development. Daily watering may be required in summer, but always wait for the soil surface to dry before watering.

Growth occurs from strong tips at the end of each branch

Origin

Native to southwestern North America, where it grows as a shrub or small tree up to 26 ft (8 m) high.

How it grows
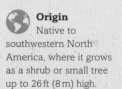
An evergreen, upright conifer, with fairly thin, brown bark and gray-green, scale-like leaves.

Position

Give it a bright position outdoors in full sun. Provide protection from long periods of freezing winter weather.

Special care
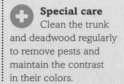
Clean the trunk and deadwood regularly to remove pests and maintain the contrast in their colors.

WIRE
Wire in spring before new growth or in fall, using copper wire. Young branches bend easily and older branches can be also be styled with care. Remove wire promptly to prevent scarring.

This yamadori *(wild-collected) tree has a slanting style*

The dark live vein is often remarkably thin

FEED

Fertilize once a month throughout the growing season using a balanced organic fertilizer to promote strong new growth.

PRUNE

Cut growing tips back in midsummer, after they have elongated. Don't pinch off new growth, or reduce the foliage mass by more than half at one pruning, as this will weaken the tree. Check where a branch's live vein leads before cutting it; with no foliage to feed the roots at its base, an area of deadwood will form. Try natural style.

REPOT

Repot every 4–5 years, in spring, once temperatures are above 41°F (5°C) and growth begins. Ideally, keep in a greenhouse (64°F/18°C) until growth resumes. Use akadama, pumice, and lava in equal parts.

Chinese juniper

Juniperus chinensis

WATER

Although drought-tolerant, water daily in summer and regularly in cooler seasons, to keep the tree developing well. Wait for the soil surface to dry before watering.

This popular bonsai species has been used to create many famous masterpieces. It has attractive compact foliage and its flexible trunk and branches often feature dramatic pale deadwood. The many varieties show nuanced differences in foliage size and color, and all make beautiful bonsai.

WIRE

Wire branches in fall or in spring, before new growth, using copper wire. Young branches are easy to mold into position, and even larger branches and the trunk can be bent. Avoid scars by removing wire in good time.

 Origin
Native to the mountains of China, Japan, Taiwan, Korea, and Myanmar, where it grows 65 ft (20 m) tall.

How it grows
Growth extends from pads of evergreen foliage along branches. The trunk can achieve wildly twisted forms.

 Position
Give it a position in full sun. Hardy, but protect trees in pots from long periods of freezing temperatures.

 Special care
Clean the trunk and deadwood regularly to check for insect pests and keep the pale color of the deadwood.

REPOT

Repot every 4–5 years, in spring once temperatures are above 41°F (5°C) and growth has begun. After repotting, keep at 64°F (18°C) until growing well. Use a soil mix of equal parts akadama, lava, and pumice.

FEED

Use a balanced organic fertilizer once a month throughout the growing season to supply the tree with the nutrients required for healthy growth.

PRUNE

Cut growing tips back in midsummer, after they have elongated. Pinching new growth too early or pruning off more than half the foliage at once weakens the tree. The raised "live vein" links foliage and roots; cutting it to remove a branch creates deadwood. Suits *kengai* (cascade) style.

This tree has been shaped into a dramatic cascade style

Rough-textured red-brown bark sets off bright green foliage

Three point display

The traditional three point display makes use of two medium-sized bonsai, with a smaller accent plant, to form a satisfying composition and increase their visual impact. The design is laid out indoors, in a small tokonoma (see p.70) or simply against a clean background, and is kept for about one week to welcome a guest or celebrate a season.

The largest tree in the display is usually a conifer, presented on a high table or stand

Select stands or tables to complement the trees and overall design of the display

One smaller accent plant shows seasonality or provides contrast with its form, texture, or leaf size

The two bonsai selected should contrast in character. Display a conifer on the high stand or table and a deciduous tree in the lower position, to mirror the altitudes of their natural habitats.

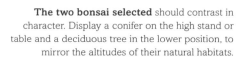

Provide a plain backdrop to accentuate the elements of the display

KEEP IT SIMPLE
Place bonsai on two small tables of different heights to form a three point display close to a window. Position your accent plant in a shallow dish on the floor.

A traditional scroll (kakejiku) can be used but is not essential in three point displays

The smaller tree is usually deciduous and takes a lower position, on a small table or polished wooden slab (jiita)

Savin juniper
Juniperus sabina

A distinctive, naturally twisted branch structure and an ability to form elegant, curvy *jins* (deadwood on branches) allows this juniper to quickly take on an aged appearance, which makes it perfect for bonsai. Choose a female specimen, because when male trees flower it reduces their growth.

This tree is shaped in literati style

WATER
Even though it is drought-resistant, regular watering is needed to keep growth strong and healthy. Water daily in summer, but always wait for the soil surface to dry and turn pale before watering again.

Origin
Native to high alpine regions in central Europe, this shrub or tree reaches 13 ft (4 m) tall with a wide canopy.

How it grows
This evergreen conifer elongates from dense tips of scale-like foliage. It has attractive pale brown bark.

WIRE
Wire in fall or before new growth in spring. Branches don't thicken rapidly and are easy to bend using copper wire. Larger branches can also be shaped. Remove wire before it scars bark.

Position
Give it a position in full sun outdoors. Protect small trees and those in pots from periods of freezing in winter.

Special care
Clean the trunk and deadwood regularly to remove pests and preserve the pale color of the deadwood.

REPOT

Repot every 4–5 years, in spring once temperatures are above 41°F (5°C) and growth has begun. After repotting, keep at 64°F (18°C) until growing well. Use a soil mix of equal parts akadama, lava, and pumice.

The pale live vein runs through the bleached deadwood

FEED

Fertilize once a month throughout the growing season using a balanced organic fertilizer to encourage the steady production of healthy new growth.

Compact fans of scale-like foliage suited to bonsai

PRUNE

Cut growing tips back in midsummer, after they have elongated. Pruning off more than half the foliage at once weakens the tree. Only pinch shoots on well developed trees. A raised live vein links foliage and roots; cutting it will form deadwood. Suits *bunjin* (literati) or *kengai* (cascade) styles.

Rocky Mountain juniper

Juniperus scopulorum

The dramatic bonsai created from this species display large deadwood features, slender live veins (portions of living bark), and scale-like foliage. Care is needed to avoid over-pruning, which will result in larger juvenile foliage.

WATER
Despite its drought resistance, water regularly to encourage good health and development. Daily watering may be needed in summer, but always allow the soil surface to dry before watering.

WIRE
Wire in fall or spring before new growth. Branches are usually easy to bend into position using copper wire. Larger branches can also be styled with care. Avoid wire scars by removing the wire in good time.

Origin
Native to the mountains of western North America, where trees reach 33–66 ft (10–20 m) high.

How it grows
A rounded, evergreen tree with textured bark and slender shoots, which elongate from strong growing tips.

Position
Give it a position outdoors in full sun all year round. Provide protection from long periods of freezing winter weather.

Special care
Clean the trunk and deadwood regularly to remove pests and keep a contrast between the deadwood and live vein.

This natural deadwood is impossible to recreate by hand

PRUNE

Cut growing tips back in midsummer, after they have elongated. Don't pinch off new growth, or remove more than half the foliage at once, as this weakens the tree. Check where a live vein leads before cutting it; with no foliage to feed the roots at its base, an area of deadwood will form. Try natural style.

FEED

Fertilize throughout the growing season, using a balanced organic fertilizer once a month.

REPOT

Repot every 4–5 years, in spring, once in growth and temperatures are above 41°F (5°C). Ideally, keep in a greenhouse (64°F/18°C) until growth resumes. Use equal parts akadama, lava, and pumice.

A rugged trunk contrasts with refined foliage and branches

European larch

Larix decidua

A handsome bonsai species that combines the powerful thick trunk, deadwood features, and luxuriant foliage of a conifer with the seasonal interest of a deciduous tree. Its slender needles turn golden yellow in fall, before falling in winter to reveal textured bark and gnarled branches.

WATER

Water regularly to keep the soil consistently moist. Avoid allowing the soil surface to dry out, because larches require a lot more water than other conifers.

Grown in the slanting style

Origin
Native to the mountains of Europe, where it grows as a tree up to 130 ft (40 m) high.

How it grows
A deciduous, upright conifer, with strong new shoots. Heals (calluses) well when cut back to old wood.

Position
Give it a position in full sun outdoors. Protect the roots from long periods of freezing in winter.

Special care
Larches like full sun, but foliage will scorch in temperatures above 86°F (30°C), when they should be given shade.

WIRE

Wire in fall or in spring before new growth appears, using copper wire. Even older branches are flexible and easy to bend into position. Branches thicken rapidly so be careful to remove wire before it causes scarring.

Delicate needles grow in attractive spiky clusters

Bark becomes cracked and fissured with age

PRUNE

Cut growing tips back in midsummer, after they have elongated. Prune branches back to a new bud pointing in the desired direction for growth. Produces shoots from the trunk when cut back to old wood, allowing the creation of new branches. In later development, pinch out new shoots to stimulate inner buds. Suits slanting or modern natural styles.

REPOT

Repot every 4–5 years, in spring once temperatures are above 41°F (5°C) and growth has begun. After repotting, keep at 64°F (18°C) until growing well. Use a soil mix of equal parts akadama, lava, and pumice.

FEED

Fertilize once a month throughout the growing season using a balanced organic fertilizer to encourage healthy growth and development.

Japanese larch

Larix kaempferi

WATER
Keep consistently moist throughout the year by watering daily in summer and less frequently during winter. Do not allow the soil surface to dry out.

This deciduous conifer is fast growing and flexible, making it an ideal choice for bonsai. Slender, needle-like foliage turns golden yellow before dropping in fall, leaving the attractive reddish brown branches and smooth bark on display during winter.

Small cones form at the ends of branches, where they can remain for several years

Origin
Native to the mountains of Japan, where trees reach up to 130 ft (40 m) high.

How it grows
An upright, conical, deciduous tree. It calluses (heals) well when cut back hard to old wood.

WIRE
Wire in fall or before new spring growth. Use copper wire. Branches bend into position easily and even older branches are flexible. Branches thicken quickly so take care to remove wire before it causes scarring.

Position
Give it a position in full sun outdoors. Protect the roots from long periods of freezing in winter.

Special care
Larches are easily scorched in temperatures above 86°F (30°C). Give them shade in hot summer weather.

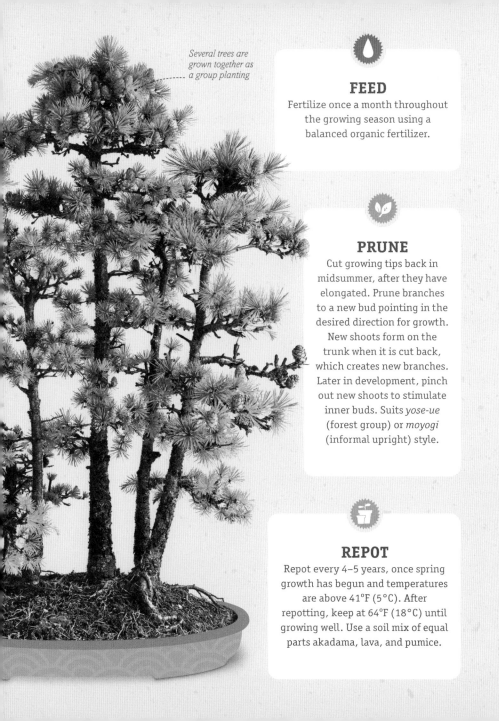

Several trees are grown together as a group planting

FEED

Fertilize once a month throughout the growing season using a balanced organic fertilizer.

PRUNE

Cut growing tips back in midsummer, after they have elongated. Prune branches to a new bud pointing in the desired direction for growth. New shoots form on the trunk when it is cut back, which creates new branches. Later in development, pinch out new shoots to stimulate inner buds. Suits *yose-ue* (forest group) or *moyogi* (informal upright) style.

REPOT

Repot every 4–5 years, once spring growth has begun and temperatures are above 41°F (5°C). After repotting, keep at 64°F (18°C) until growing well. Use a soil mix of equal parts akadama, lava, and pumice.

Dwarf crab apple

Malus spp.

The seasonal highlights of delicate late spring blossom and colorful fall fruits, make the crab apple an attractive and rewarding bonsai to grow. *Malus cerasifera* and *M. sylvestris* are most commonly grown as bonsai, and many other varieties with particularly small fruit also make beautiful specimens.

WATER
These thirsty plants need a lot of water, particularly in spring. Keep soil constantly moist by watering up to twice a day in hot summer weather. Hard tap water is ideal; it may be necessary to add a lime supplement if rainwater is used.

Pink or white, cup-like flowers precede the fruits

Origin
Native to Asia, Europe, and North America, where they grow up to 13 ft (4 m) tall, with wide canopies.

How it grows
This rounded, deciduous tree has alternating, heart-shaped, serrated leaves. The fruits often remain into winter.

WIRE
Wire bare branches in fall or in spring before growth, using aluminum wire. Younger shoots are easy to bend into position, but older branches tend to break. Avoid wire scars by removing wire before it damages the branch.

Position
Give it full sun or semi-shade outdoors. Move into a greenhouse or a cool, bright room, for protection in winter.

Special care
Grow two crab apple bonsai close to each other to increase the chances of pollination and the number of fruit.

This tree has been styled as an informal upright

A thick trunk balances relatively large leaves

FEED

Fertilize once a month throughout the growing season, using a balanced organic feed. To promote flowers, avoid high-nitrogen feeds at the beginning and end of the growing season.

PRUNE

Prune in early summer, after new leaves have "hardened off" (turned darker and toughened). This encourages the formation of buds back from the shoot tip, and branching. Pinch out in later stages to refine branches at the edge of the canopy. Try *moyogi* (informal upright) style.

REPOT

Repot every 4–5 years, in spring before growth begins. Prune the roots to produce a strong *nebari* (root-flare). Use pure akadama to retain water at the roots.

European olive

Olea europaea

WATER

Although drought-tolerant, olives consume a lot of water on hot days. Regular watering is essential for trees in shallow pots. Water up to twice a day in hot summer weather and less frequently in cooler conditions.

Thick, dark green leaves contrast with the light, deadwood features on dramatic old trunks, to give this tough evergreen species its unique character. The wild olive (*O. e.* subsp. *europaea* var. *sylvestris*) makes the best bonsai specimens, as its leaves are smaller and have shorter internodes than cultivated species, producing desirable, compact foliage.

WIRE

Wire branches after pruning or before new growth in spring. Use aluminum wire. Young branches are easy to bend into position, but older branches are brittle. Avoid wire scars by removing wire in good time.

 Origin
Native to Mediterranean regions of Europe, where trees can reach 65 ft (20 m) tall.

 How it grows
An evergreen, rounded tree with alternating, leathery leaves. Trees rarely flower and fruit as bonsai.

 Position
Give it a position in full sun outdoors. It can tolerate light frosts, but trees in pots are best kept indoors during winter.

 Special care
To increase the longevity of deadwood, clean and care for it once a year with a wire brush.

A small pot alludes to tough conditions faced by the tree

Tree shaped into the slender literati style

A strong nebari *creates a sense of stability*

REPOT

Repot every 4–5 years, before growth starts in spring. Prune roots to produce a strong *nebari* (root-flare). Use a moisture-retentive soil mix containing equal parts akadama and lava or pumice.

FEED

Fertilize once a month throughout the growing season using a balanced organic fertilizer, to promote healthy growth.

PRUNE

Prune in midsummer to promote branching. Pinching out shoots also encourages branching by directing energy to buds further back on the branch. Olives callus (heal) poorly, so large cuts on the trunk should be left as stumps to turn into deadwood. Suits *bunjin* (literati) and *moyogi* (informal upright) styles.

Ezo spruce

Picea jezoensis

This distinguished evergreen conifer has been molded into many famous Japanese bonsai. It is revered for the density of its branching and foliage, as well as the small size of its shoots and needles. These are readily produced with the correct care, and form foliage pads with superb refinement and definition.

WATER
Keep consistently moist by watering regularly throughout the year, never allowing the soil surface to dry out.

WIRE
Wire branches in fall or in spring before new growth appears, using copper wire. Even older branches remain flexible and are easy to bend into position. Avoid scars by removing the wire in good time.

🌍 Origin
Native to the mountains of Japan, China, North Korea, and Siberia, where trees reach 164 ft (50 m) high.

 How it grows
An evergreen conifer with textured bark. Shoots elongate most vigorously from brown buds at branch tips.

☀ Position
Give it a position in full sun or semi-shade outdoors. Hardy enough to remain outdoors throughout winter.

 Special care
Adapted to cool climates, place these trees under a shade cloth when summer temperatures rise above 86°F (30°C).

Young foliage adds a flush of lighter green in spring

REPOT

Repot every 4–5 years, in spring, once temperatures are above 41°F (5°C) and growth begins. Ideally, keep in a greenhouse (64°F/18°C) until growth resumes. Use equal parts akadama, pumice, and lava.

PRUNE

To increase branch density, pinch off new growth in mid-spring as it elongates, but before needles open out. Where many shoots grow from one location (node), thin them in late spring, once shoots have "hardened off" (darkened), to leave two shoots per node. Try *sokan* (upright) and *shakan* (slanting) styles.

The slanting style of the tree is counterbalanced with a tall rock

FEED

Feed once a month using a balanced organic fertilizer throughout the growing season.

Mountain pine

Pinus mugo

Robust and flexible, this evergreen conifer is well-suited to bonsai. It is often styled to combine a powerful trunk, characterized by dramatic movement, deadwood, and rugged bark, with elegant pads of strong, short needles.

WATER
Water regularly, but always allow the soil surface to dry out between waterings to avoid over watering this drought-tolerant species.

WIRE
Wire the flexible branches in fall or before new growth appears in spring. Use copper wire. The trunk and larger branches also remain flexible enough to style with care. Remove wire before it damages the branch to avoid scarring.

Origin
Native to the mountains of northern and central Europe, they can form wide, low canopies at altitude.

How it grows
A rounded, slow-growing, evergreen tree with textured, gray bark and large, sticky winter buds at each branch tip.

Position
Place outdoors in full sun throughout the year. Protect from long periods of freezing weather in winter.

Special care
This alpine tree is hardy and drought-tolerant, but is weakened by over watering during fall and winter.

The stumps of pruned branches form jins

This young tree is being shaped into slanting style

FEED

Fertilize once a month throughout the growing season using balanced organic fertilizer, to help promote healthy growth.

PRUNE

Prune in midsummer, once new shoots are fully developed and the young needles have turned dark. For a compact form, prune to leave a short portion of new growth. Pinch stem tips to stimulate growth of back buds (buds away from the tip) and to form dense pads of needles. Suits *shakan* (slanting) and natural styles.

REPOT

Repot every 4–5 years, depending on the rate of development, in spring before growth begins. Use a well-aerated soil mix containing equal parts of akadama, lava, and pumice.

Shohin display

Small bonsai up to 8 in (20 cm) tall are known as *shohin* and are traditionally displayed as a group arranged on a special stand, with a separate accompanying tree on its own stand, and an accent plant. They often honor a visitor or a season in the same way as other traditional displays.

Provide a plain backdrop to accentuate the elements of the display

A separate stand holds a tree in a cascade or slanting style, the defining branch of which points toward the main stand

An accent plant is placed between the two stands at the center of the display

Classical shohin displays are presented indoors for a short period in a small tokonoma (see p.70) or against a clean background. They are also a popular way for enthusiasts to display their best small bonsai at exhibitions.

The top tree should be a conifer species native to high altitudes and usually has a masculine form

A classical shohin display stand usually holds five trees, each presented at a different level

Arrange coniferous or deciduous species naturally found at higher altitudes on the first level

Position deciduous trees on the ground level, which also suits multi-trunk or forest styles

Japanese white pine

Pinus parviflora

A classic of Japanese bonsai, known throughout the world for the striking, strong, traditional forms that it can create. It has beautiful gray bark and small, soft needles, which often display a bluish tinge as a result of being grafted onto a black pine rootstock.

A dramatic windswept style suits this pine

WATER
Be careful to avoid over watering this drought-tolerant tree. Always allow the soil surface to dry between waterings, but never let the soil dry out completely.

 Origin
Native to Japan, growing at altitudes of up to 5,900 ft (1,800 m), where trees can reach 82 ft (25 m) tall.

 How it grows
This slow-growing, evergreen conifer forms needles in bundles of five. Shoots elongate from buds at branch tips.

 Position
Give it a position in full sun outdoors, year-round. Protect from heavy rainfall in winter.

 Special care
Too much water will weaken this otherwise robust pine in temperate climates, especially in fall and winter.

WIRE
Wire the flexible branches in fall or spring before new growth, using copper wire. The trunk and larger branches can also be shaped with care. Avoid wire scars by removing wire before it damages the branch.

PRUNE

Prune in summer, once the new shoots are fully developed and the young needles emerge. Cut back this young growth each year, leaving a short portion of the new shoot. Suits all styles; try *moyogi* (informal upright) or *fukinagashi* (windswept).

REPOT

Repot every 4–5 years in spring, before new growth begins. Use a well-aerated soil mix containing equal proportions of akadama, lava, and pumice.

A jin *(deadwood feature) provides a counterbalance to the canopy*

FEED

Fertilize once a month throughout the growing season using a balanced organic fertilizer.

Ponderosa pine

Pinus ponderosa

This species has only recently gained popularity as a bonsai, because the size of its long, fleshy needles can make it tough to work with. However, beautifully ramified (finely branched) ponderosa pines, with medium-sized needles, gnarled deadwood, and rugged bark, now epitomize modern natural bonsai.

WATER

Be careful not to over water. Water regularly, but always allow the soil surface to dry between waterings.

This yamadori (wild-collected) tree has beautiful natural twists in its trunk

 Origin
Native to the Rocky Mountains in western North America, where trees reach a huge 230 ft (70 m) high.

 How it grows
A conical, evergreen conifer, with dark bark and shoots that elongate from buds at the end of each branch.

WIRE

Wire the flexible branches in fall or in spring before new growth, using copper wire. The shape of the trunk and larger branches can also be manipulated with care. Avoid scars by removing wire in good time.

 Position
Give it a position outdoors year-round in full sun. Protect from heavy rainfall and freezing weather in winter.

 Special care
Too much water can weaken this drought-tolerant tree in temperate climates, especially during fall and winter.

FEED

Fertilize once a month throughout the growing season, using a balanced organic fertilizer, to fuel healthy growth.

REPOT

Repot every 4–5 years, in spring before new growth appears. Use a well-aerated soil mix, containing equal proportions of akadama, lava, and pumice, to provide the excellent drainage that this tree needs at its roots.

PRUNE

In summer, once the new shoots are fully developed and new needles have darkened, prune the young growth back, leaving a short portion of the new shoot. This promotes branch formation. Suits all bonsai styles; try natural.

Planting off-center balances the sweeping form of the tree

Scots pine

Pinus sylvestris

This tough species responds well to bonsai cultivation and is easy to care for, which makes it an ideal choice for beginners. Its natural combination of elegant lines; textured bark; and fine, short needles creates beautiful bonsai, especially in the tall *bunjin* (literati) style with its bare trunk, shown in this example.

WATER
Water regularly, but always allow the soil surface to dry before watering. Check daily during summer and less frequently in winter.

WIRE
Wire the flexible branches in fall or before new growth in spring. Use copper wire. The trunk and larger branches also remain flexible enough to style with care. Avoid scars by removing wire before it bites into the wood.

Origin
Native to diverse habitats in Europe and temperate Asia, trees can reach up to 130 ft (40 m) high.

How it grows
A conical, rather slow-growing, evergreen tree with flaking red-brown bark and blue-green needles.

Position
Give it a position in full sun outdoors. Fully hardy, but protect from long periods of freezing winter weather.

Special care
Although robust and hardy, this tree can be damaged by over watering during fall and winter.

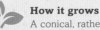

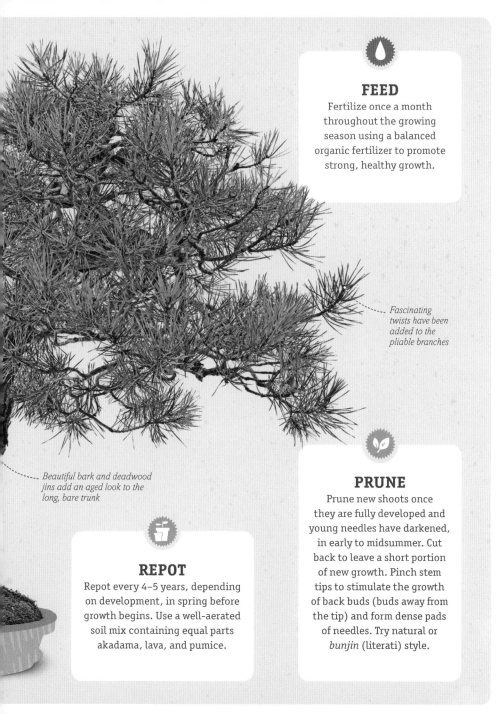

FEED

Fertilize once a month throughout the growing season using a balanced organic fertilizer to promote strong, healthy growth.

Fascinating twists have been added to the pliable branches

Beautiful bark and deadwood jins add an aged look to the long, bare trunk

REPOT

Repot every 4–5 years, depending on development, in spring before growth begins. Use a well-aerated soil mix containing equal parts akadama, lava, and pumice.

PRUNE

Prune new shoots once they are fully developed and young needles have darkened, in early to midsummer. Cut back to leave a short portion of new growth. Pinch stem tips to stimulate the growth of back buds (buds away from the tip) and form dense pads of needles. Try natural or *bunjin* (literati) style.

Japanese black pine

Pinus thunbergii

Perhaps the embodiment of a classic bonsai pine, the Japanese black pine's compact form; dark bark; powerful movement; and pads of dense, long, sharp needles all combine to create trees with a great sense of age and immense character.

WATER

Water regularly, but always allow the soil surface to dry before watering. Check daily during summer and less frequently at other times of the year.

WIRE

Use copper wire to shape the flexible branches in fall or before new growth in spring. The trunk and larger branches also remain flexible enough to style with care. Remove wire in good time to avoid scarring.

Origin

Native to warm, humid, coastal areas of Japan and South Korea, where trees can reach 130 ft (40 m) tall.

How it grows

A strong-growing, conical, evergreen conifer, with thick, gray-green needle-like leaves and dark purple-gray bark.

Position

Give it a position in full sun outdoors. Provide protection if temperatures fall below 14°F (−10°C) for prolonged periods.

Special care

Careful pruning and feeding is needed to reduce needle size and increase branching, so not ideal for beginners.

REPOT

Repot every 4–5 years, in spring before growth begins. Use a well-aerated soil mix containing equal parts of akadama, lava, and pumice.

FEED

Feed from the first spring growth until shoots are cut back in early summer. Begin feeding again when the second flush of growth has hardened off in late summer and continue until winter.

PRUNE

If trees are strong and healthy, remove new shoots completely as they start to open and show their needles in early summer. This gives a second flush of growth with more ramification (branching) and shorter needles. Suits *moyogi* (informal upright) and *bunjin* (literati) styles.

Manage spiky clusters of foliage to allow light into the center of the canopy

The literati style shows the pine's rugged bark to dramatic effect

Manila tamarind

Pithecellobium dulce

An exotic beauty, the wonderful gray, fine-barked trunk and small leaves of the Manila tamarind make it an ideal bonsai specimen, which can be grown indoors. It also produces fragrant, white spring flowers and deliciously scented pods containing edible pulp.

WATER
Avoid over watering by checking daily during growth and only watering when the soil surface is dry. Water less often in winter.

WIRE
Wire branches after pruning or before spring growth, using aluminum wire. Young branches bend readily, but older branches break easily. Avoid wire scars by removing wire in good time.

 Origin
Native to Mexico, Central America, and northern South America, where trees grow up to 49 ft (15 m) tall.

 How it grows
A vigorous, evergreen tree with small, leathery leaves and colorful, twisted pendent fruits.

 Position
Give it full sun outdoors in summer. Keep indoors in winter, or all year in cool areas, in a bright spot at 59°F (15°C).

 Special care
Water sparingly in winter and keep the tree protected from heavy rainfall to prevent the soil remaining too wet.

Pods turn pink and start to split open when ripe

FEED

Fertilize once a month throughout the growing season using a balanced organic fertilizer.

PRUNE

The strong growth of this species can be pruned hard. Prune new shoots back to two buds once they have "hardened off" (toughened and darkened) in mid- to late spring. Suits natural and *yose-ue* (group planting) styles.

REPOT

Repot every 3–4 years, in spring before growth. Prune roots to form a good *nebari* (root-flare). Use a 1:1 mix of akadama and lava or pumice.

Naturally compact, the glossy foliage is well-suited to bonsai

This forest group emphasizes the pale bark and nebari

Blackthorn

Prunus spinosa

This hardy tree is trouble-free to care for as a bonsai and will readily produce a finely branched specimen that is full of character. It is grown for the beautiful contrast between its small, white, fragrant spring flowers, and the dark bark of its trunk and spiny branches. The delicate leaves also turn red in fall, as the fruit (sloes) ripen.

WATER

Keep soil consistently moist by watering regularly. Shallow bonsai pots may need watering as often as twice a day in hot summer weather, but less frequently in cooler conditions.

WIRE

Wire young shoots in fall or in spring before new growth appears. Use aluminum wire. Older branches are stiff and hard to bend without breaking. Avoid scars by removing wire before it damages the branch.

Origin
Native to Europe, the Mediterranean, and North Africa, where shrubs or trees can reach 20 ft (6 m) high.

How it grows
A deciduous tree or shrub, with spring blossom and black fruit. Oddly angled shoots form bizarrely shaped bonsai.

Position
Give it a position in full sun or semi-shade outdoors, where it is best protected from heavy frosts.

Special care
Be careful to avoid injury on the strong thorns when pruning. It is best to remove fruits to avoid exhausting the tree.

REPOT

Repot every 3–4 years, according to the tree's development, in spring before growth begins. Use a moisture-retentive mix containing equal ratios of akadama and lava or pumice.

Leave sloes on the tree to ripen to dark purple in fall

FEED

Fertilize throughout the growing season, but to ensure a good display of flowers, avoid using high-nitrogen fertilizers in spring and fall.

This tree is shaped in the literati style

PRUNE

Prune to create a good structure and even growth. In early summer, prune hard to achieve good ramification (branching). Leave the stumps of pruned branches on the trunk to form deadwood, as cuts do not callus (heal) well on pot-grown trees. Suits all styles; try *bunjin* (literati) and fairytale.

Chinese quince

Pseudocydonia sinensis

A star performer, with color all year round, this deciduous tree boasts elegant dark green, serrated leaves, pale pink spring flowers, large yellow fruit, and golden fall color. Its outstanding feature however is its flaky bark, which creates a unique camouflage-like effect.

WATER

Water carefully to keep soil constantly moist. Water twice a day in hot summer weather, particularly when grown in a shallow pot. Reduce watering in cooler conditions, but continue to keep soil moist.

Five-petaled flowers are a spring highlight

 Origin
Native to East Asia, where trees can grow up to 20 ft (6 m) tall in temperate woodland.

 How it grows
This deciduous tree produces strong elongating shoots, carrying alternating tapered leaves.

Position
Best in a bright, sunny spot. Trees will tolerate semi-shade, but produce less spectacular fall color.

 Special care
Although it is hardy, providing winter protection under cover results in much more vigorous spring growth.

WIRE

Wire bare branches in fall after leaf drop or in spring before the new growth appears. Use aluminum wire. Wire scars should be avoided by removing the wire in good time.

PRUNE

Prune back secondary branches hard in midsummer to create a good structure of finer branches and a dense canopy. Avoid large cuts on main branches along the trunk as they callus (heal) poorly. Suits all styles; try *sokan* (twin-trunk) or *kabudachi* (clump).

Multiple trunks arise from one base in the clump style

FEED

Apply a balanced organic fertilizer monthly throughout the growing season. Avoid high-nitrogen feeds at the beginning and end of the growing season to promote flowering.

REPOT

Repot every 3–4 years in spring, before growth starts. Use a moisture-retentive soil mix containing equal proportions of akadama and lava or pumice.

English oak

Quercus robur

This iconic European species makes memorable bonsai, with its distinctive lobed leaves; thick, powerful, upright trunk; and spreading branches. Its form will never be as refined as some more traditional deciduous bonsai species, but it can convey age and strength beautifully.

WATER

Keep consistently moist and never allow the soil to dry out. Water specimens kept in shallow pots up to twice a day in hot summer weather and check them regularly throughout the rest of the year.

Large leaves can be reduced in size as the tree matures and its growth is refined

Origin
Native to the temperate regions of Europe, where trees can reach heights of up to 130 ft (40 m).

How it grows
A spreading, deciduous tree, with fissured gray-brown bark, lobed leaves, and good fall color.

Position
Give it a position in full sun outdoors, with good air circulation. Protect from long periods of hard frosts in winter.

Special care
Susceptible to the fungal infection, mildew. Provide good ventilation to keep the leaves dry and healthy.

WIRE

Wire young shoots in fall or in spring before new growth appears. Use aluminum wire. Older branches are stiff and hard to bend without breaking. Avoid scars by removing wire before it damages the branch.

FEED

Fertilize throughout the growing season by applying a balanced organic fertilizer once a month, which will support strong and healthy growth.

PRUNE

Prune back the shoot from the strongest central bud at the branch tip, to allow other back buds (buds further down the stem) to grow and create branching. Leave stumps of pruned branches on the trunk to form deadwood, as cuts do not callus (heal) well. Try *moyogi* (informal upright) and fairytale styles.

A strong nebari (root-flare) and thick trunk add to the tree's sturdy character

REPOT

Repot every 3–4 years, depending on development, before growth begins in spring. Use a moisture-retentive mix containing akadama and lava or pumice in equal ratios, to keep roots supplied with water.

Outdoor display

Most bonsai are grown outdoors year-round, so it makes sense to present them in an attractive way. Poles and benches are both used to bring trees closer to eye level, making it easier to maintain them and admire their detail. There is no formal tradition of outdoor bonsai display, which leaves you free to express your creativity.

A wooden fence is a practical boundary and an excellent contrasting background for bonsai

Top benches and poles with wood, as ceramic pots chip easily on harder materials

Construct benches from wood, metal, or stone, ensuring that they can hold the weight of your trees

Benches are a simple way to display developing trees above ground level. More mature bonsai are often presented on poles. Vary the height of display platforms to suit each tree's style and help provide ideal conditions.

Secure the pot to the platform to prevent your bonsai toppling off in high winds

TIGHT FOR SPACE
A garden wall or fence makes a good backdrop for small bonsai on shelves. Create a striking pattern of shelves, inspired by a shohin display (see p.106), to use limited space efficiently.

The platform on top of the pole should be just large enough to hold the bonsai pot

Sturdy poles can be made of wood, concrete, natural stone, or metal

Cover the base of the pole with simple plants, such as grasses, to integrate it into the garden

Satsuki azalea

Rhododendron indicum cvs

Special bonsai exhibitions dedicated to these powerhouses of late spring and early summer blooms show the huge variety of flower color and size found among satsuki cultivars. 'Jukokan' produces a mass of fine, candy pink flowers. Satsukis are easy to style, but need moist, acidic soil, and soft water.

WATER

Keep consistently moist and never allow the soil to dry out. Water with soft rainwater up to twice a day in hot summer weather and regularly, but less frequently, in cooler conditions.

FEED

Begin feeding after flowering, in early summer, and continue until the end of the growing season. Use a balanced organic fertilizer once a month.

 **Origin**
Native to the mountains of Japan, where they grow as wide shrubs to 6 ft (2 m) tall.

 How it grows
An evergreen, with glossy leaves and funnel-shaped flowers. Several shoots arise at the base of each spent bloom.

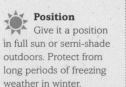 **Position**
Give it a position in full sun or semi-shade outdoors. Protect from long periods of freezing weather in winter.

 **Special care**
A robust and hardy bonsai when well cared for, but prone to pests and diseases if kept too dry or watered with hard water.

REPOT

Repot every 2–4 years, in early spring before growth. Use special Japanese azalea compost called *kanuma* to provide the right moist, acidic conditions for the fine roots.

WIRE

Wire and bend the young shoots in fall or in spring before new growth appears, using aluminum wire. Older branches are stiff and hard to bend without breaking. Wire scars should be avoided by removing the wire before it damages the branch.

PRUNE

This species can be pruned hard and forms fine branches well. Start pruning in mid- to late summer, once new growth has "hardened off" (toughened and darkened). Lower branches tend to be more vigorous than those higher up, so prune lightly at the apex and more heavily toward the base. Try *chokkan* (upright) style.

Pretty pink flowers also look attractive in bud

Shaped in a formal upright style, with asymmetrical branches

Sageretia

Sageretia thea

This frost-tender, evergreen tree is a popular choice for indoor bonsai. Its delicate, soft leaves; clusters of white flowers; blue berries; and light-colored bark provide year-round seasonal interest. It reacts well to pruning and rapidly forms an attractive structure of fine branches.

WATER

Water regularly to keep the soil consistently moist, but always let the soil surface dry between waterings. Check daily during periods of hot summer weather.

The subtle flowers are followed by edible fruits

Origin
Native to China, Myanmar, and eastern India, where trees reach 6–10 ft (2–3 m) high.

How it grows
This bushy evergreen grows vigorously and is easy to style into a beautiful dense, shape.

Position
Needs full sun in the growing season. Keep indoors where summers are cool, at a temperature of around 68°F (20°C).

Special care
High humidity is required year-round. Keep indoor plants away from direct heat sources and mist daily.

WIRE

Wire and bend the young shoots year-round, using aluminum wire. Older branches with thicker bark are stiff and difficult to bend without breaking. Wire scars should be avoided by removing the wire before it damages the wood.

FEED

Fertilize throughout the entire year, because the tree is always growing. Use a balanced organic fertilizer once a month.

REPOT

Repot every 3 years in spring. Add a drainage layer of bigger lava or pumice to the base of the pot and fill with a soil mix of equal parts akadama and lava or pumice.

This bonsai has been grown as a twin-trunk with a wide canopy

PRUNE

Allow new growth to "harden off" (toughen and darken in color) in early summer, before pruning it back to two leaves. Continue to prune to shape throughout the year. As the fine branching becomes denser, start pinching out shoot tips. Suits *sokan* (twin-trunk) and *yose-ue* (forest planting).

Coastal redwood

Sequoia sempervirens

One of the world's tallest tree species in the wild, the coastal redwood's naturally straight habit lends itself to upright bonsai styles. *Yamadori* (wild-collected) specimens often possess spectacular deadwood features, however, which provide scope to create a much stockier, more gnarled image.

WATER
Water daily in summer, and regularly during cooler times of year, to keep the soil evenly moist. Don't allow the soil surface to dry out.

Elegant branches carry feather-like stems of needles

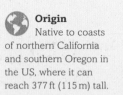

Origin
Native to coasts of northern California and southern Oregon in the US, where it can reach 377 ft (115 m) tall.

How it grows
An evergreen with flat needles borne on shoots along, and at the tips, of branches. Old wood also bears shoots.

Position
Give it a bright position in full sun outdoors during the growing season.

Special care
Provide humidity year-round and protection from cold winds in winter, either in a greenhouse or cool room indoors.

WIRE
Wire branches in fall or in spring before growth, using copper wire. Older branches are stiffer and hard to bend, but can also be shaped with care. Remove wire promptly, as branches thicken rapidly.

*Red-brown bark
becomes rough
as it matures*

FEED

Fertilize once a month during the growing season using a balanced organic fertilizer. Switch to a low-nitrogen feed in early fall to improve hardiness.

PRUNE

In early summer, prune back to new buds on the underside of branches, which point in the desired direction of growth. Cut back to old wood to promote new shoots from old parts of the trunk. In later development, pinch new elongating shoots to direct energy to inner buds. Suits *chokkan* (upright) style.

REPOT

Repot every 3–5 years, once spring growth has begun and it is consistently above 41°F (5°C). Ideally, keep in a greenhouse at 64°F (18°C) until growth resumes. Use equal parts akadama, lava, and pumice.

Tamarisk

Tamarix chinensis

Fine, feathery foliage and frothy
heads of tiny, pink spring flowers
give this species a distinctive airy
grace that works well in bonsai.
The attractive, textured bark
is often accompanied on the trunk
by carved deadwood features, which
add interest and the impression
of great age.

WATER
This is a thirsty tree
which may need watering
twice a day in hot summer
weather and regularly
throughout the year. Keep
the soil constantly moist.

*Wispy foliage is perfectly
suited to the scale of a
bonsai tree*

Origin
Native to China,
where it grows in coastal,
dry, and marshy areas.
Trees can reach up to
39 ft (12 m) in height.

How it grows
A strong-growing,
deciduous tree, with tiny
scale-like leaves and
loose flower heads
on weeping branches.

WIRE
Wire branches after
cutting back or in spring
before new growth appears,
using aluminum wire.
Branches don't thicken
quickly, and are easy to
bend into position. Older,
thicker branches are
brittle. Wire scars should
be avoided by removing
the wire in good time.

Position
Give it a position
in full sun outdoors.
Move to a bright, cool
(min. 41°F/5°C) place
under cover in winter.

Special care
Clean deadwood
and treat it with lime
sulfur once a year
to prevent it becoming
rotten with watering.

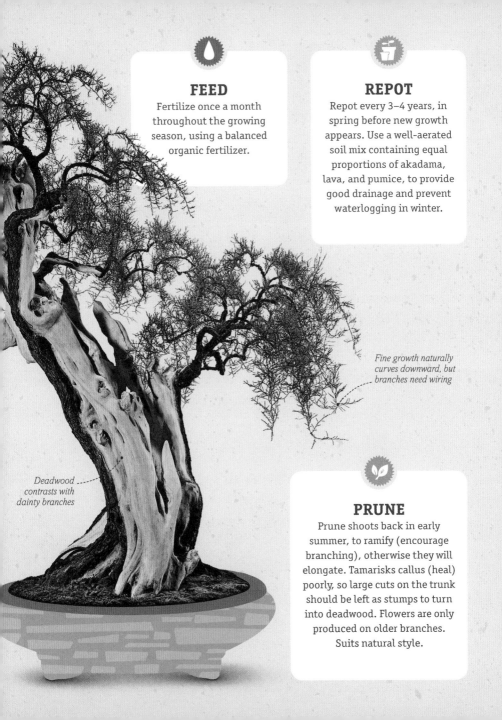

FEED
Fertilize once a month throughout the growing season, using a balanced organic fertilizer.

REPOT
Repot every 3–4 years, in spring before new growth appears. Use a well-aerated soil mix containing equal proportions of akadama, lava, and pumice, to provide good drainage and prevent waterlogging in winter.

Fine growth naturally curves downward, but branches need wiring

Deadwood contrasts with dainty branches

PRUNE
Prune shoots back in early summer, to ramify (encourage branching), otherwise they will elongate. Tamarisks callus (heal) poorly, so large cuts on the trunk should be left as stumps to turn into deadwood. Flowers are only produced on older branches. Suits natural style.

English yew

Taxus baccata

This long-lived species produces dense pads of small, glossy, dark green needles, even from the oldest parts of the trunk. Aged trunks are often full of indentations and twists, and display a startling contrast between the russet live bark and pale gray deadwood. The foliage, bark, and seeds are all toxic.

WATER

Water regularly, up to twice daily in hot summer weather, to keep the soil consistently moist. Don't allow the soil surface to dry out completely.

WIRE

Wire branches in fall or in spring before new growth, using copper wire. Older branches are less flexible, but can be wired and shaped with care. Branches thicken rapidly, so remove wire promptly to avoid scarring.

 Origin
Native to Europe and North Africa, trees can reach 66 ft (20 m) tall or adopt shrub-like forms at altitude.

 How it grows
This evergreen, broad, conical tree forms shoots that elongate from along the length and the tips of branches.

 Position
Give it a position in full sun or semi-shade outdoors. Protect roots from freezing in cold winter weather.

 Special care
Don't abruptly move trees from shade to full sun: gradually increase periods in the sun through the growing season.

REPOT

Repot every 3–5 years, in spring once growth has begun and temperatures are consistently above 41°F (5°C). Ideally, keep in a greenhouse at 64°F (18°C) until growth resumes. Use a soil mix of equal parts akadama, lava, and pumice.

FEED

Feed monthly during growth, using a balanced organic fertilizer. Switch to a low-nitrogen feed in early fall.

Dense foliage pads balance this informal upright shape

Deadwood has been bleached to lighten its color

The live vein connects foliage and roots

PRUNE

Cut the growing tips back in early summer, once they have elongated. Prune back to buds on the underside of branches, which point in the desired direction of growth. Yew forms new shoots when cut back to old parts of the trunk. In later development, pinch growing shoots to stimulate inner buds. Try natural style.

Japanese yew

Taxus cuspidata

This robust species is well-suited to cultivation as an outdoor bonsai. Its small, dark green needles emerge in every direction and can even grow from old parts of the trunk. Mature trunks exude character, with textured bark and contrasting silvery deadwood. The foliage, bark, and seeds are all toxic.

WATER

Water regularly, up to twice a day in hot summer weather, to keep the soil consistently moist. Don't allow the soil surface to dry out.

REPOT

Repot every 3–5 years, once in growth and spring temperatures stay over 41°F (5°C). Ideally, keep in a greenhouse (64°F/18°C) until growth resumes. Use equal parts akadama, pumice, and lava.

PRUNE

Cut growing tips back in early summer, once they have elongated. Prune to buds on the underside of branches, which point in the desired direction of growth. Cut back to old wood on the trunk to form new shoots. In later development, pinch out shoots to stimulate inner buds. Try *moyogi* (informal upright) style.

 Origin
Native to Japan and northeast China, where trees can reach up to 52 ft (16 m) in height.

 How it grows
A columnar evergreen tree with shoots that elongate from buds along the length of branches and at their tips.

 **Position**
Give it a position in full sun or semi-shade outdoors. Protect roots from freezing in cold winter weather.

 Special care
Don't abruptly move trees from shade to full sun: gradually increase periods in the sun through the growing season.

WIRE

Wire branches in fall or in spring before new growth, using copper wire. Older branches are less flexible, but can be wired and shaped with care. Branches thicken rapidly, so remove wire promptly to avoid scarring.

FEED

Fertilize once a month during the growing season using a balanced organic feed. Switch to a low-nitrogen feed in early fall to improve hardiness.

Shari deadwood dominates the trunk, with a thin live vein

Lighter green foliage marks the Japanese yew out from its European relative

Chinese elm

Ulmus parvifolia

This elegant, deciduous tree is suitable for growing as an indoor bonsai and its toughness makes it ideal for beginners. Its tiny, serrated leaves, excellent ramification (structure of fine branches), and often interesting trunks, readily produce bonsai with perfect proportions, and it suits many styles.

WATER

Water regularly, up to twice a day in hot summer weather, to keep the soil consistently moist. This species tends to lose its leaves if kept too dry.

This elegant tree is in the informal upright style

Origin
Native to East Asia, where trees can reach up to 66 ft (20 m) in height.

How it grows
This spreading, deciduous tree produces shoots over the entire canopy and can even form shoots on old wood.

Position
Provide full sun, outdoors or indoors, for the growing season. In winter, keep in a cool, bright spot indoors.

Special care
Evergreen when kept at high temperatures (68°F/20°C) indoors, but healthier given winter rest at 41–50°F (5–10°C).

FEED

Fertilize once a month throughout the growing season, using a balanced organic fertilizer.

WIRE

Wire young branches after pruning in early summer, in winter after leaf-fall, or in spring before new growth, using aluminum wire. Older branches tend to break. Avoid scars by removing wire in good time.

PRUNE

Prune back to ramify (form fine branches) in late spring to early summer and, if a flush of new shoots forms, prune again in midsummer. Don't prune later, as new growth won't "harden off" (toughen) for winter. Pinch to ramify further. Try *moyogi* (informal upright) and *sokan* (twin-trunk) styles.

A strong nebari *(root-flare) adds a sense of age*

REPOT

Repot every 3 years, in spring before growth begins. Prune roots to help produce a strong *nebari* (root-flare). Use a water-retentive mix of equal parts akadama and lava or pumice.

Japanese elm

Zelkova serrata

With its elegant, tapering, serrated leaves and incredibly fine branching, this vigorous tree quickly develops an excellent shape. These characteristics naturally lend themselves to the broom style, so the Japanese elm is almost always grown in this way, with branches fanning out at the top of a straight trunk.

WATER
Water regularly, up to twice a day during hot summer weather, to keep the soil evenly moist. Elms tend to lose their leaves if kept too dry, so check trees in shallow pots frequently.

FEED
Fertilize once a month throughout the growing season. Use a balanced organic fertilizer.

Origin
Native to Japan, Korea, eastern China, and Taiwan, where trees reach 100 ft (30 m) tall.

How it grows
This fast-growing, deciduous tree produces a dense canopy of foliage with rich fall color.

Position
Give it a position in full sun outdoors. Move into a greenhouse or cool room indoors for winter protection.

Special care
Although it is hardy, this tree is best kept under cover in winter, to protect its thin branches from the cold.

WIRE
Wire young branches after pruning in early summer, in winter after leaf-fall, or in spring before growth, using aluminum wire. Older branches tend to break. Avoid scars by removing wire in good time.

Bright, lime green leaves turn a deep yellow in fall

This informal upright style boasts a sturdy, straight trunk

PRUNE

Cut back to ramify (form fine branches) in late spring or early summer and, if a flush of new shoots is formed, prune again in midsummer. Don't prune later, as new growth won't have time to "harden off" (toughen) for winter. Pinch to ramify further. Try *chokkan* (upright) or broom style.

REPOT

Repot every 3 years, in spring before growth begins. Prune roots every time you repot to help form a strong *nebari* (root-flare). Use a water-retentive mix of equal parts akadama and lava or pumice.

INDEX

ABOUT THE AUTHOR

Michael Tran owns and runs his own bonsai nursery in Germany, where he specializes in European bonsai species. Born in 1982, he began his bonsai training with Mr. Udo Fischer, and had the chance to meet and learn from Japanese masters while under his wing. After two years he became self-taught, and his mastery of bonsai at a young age led him to be called a prodigy. Today he is honored to have some of Europe's oldest, prize-winning masterpieces in his care, which have been passed down to him from the first generation of European bonsai practitioners. Michael has published many articles in bonsai magazines, and gives lectures, workshops, and demonstrations all over Europe.

AUTHOR'S ACKNOWLEDGMENTS

My thanks go to Jo Whittingham and Alastair Laing for their hard work. Seeing their ever-growing enthusiasm for bonsai has been awesome. I hope that this book enables them, and everyone who reads it, to become more aware of the trees and natural world around them, because there is a big difference between just looking at a tree and really seeing it.

PUBLISHER'S ACKNOWLEDGMENTS

DK would like to thank US consultant Mark Fields (Bonsai by Fields; president, American Bonsai Society), Ian Cuppleditch for his generous assistance with the photography, and Marie Lorimer for indexing. DK Delhi would like to thank Aashirwad Jain for editorial assistance and Vikas Sachdeva for design assistance.

Picture credits

The publisher would like to thank the following for kind permission to reproduce their photographs:

(Key: a-above; b-below/bottom; c-center; f-far; l-left; r-right; t-top)

1 Dorling Kindersley: Will Heap / John Brocklehurst. **4 Dorling Kindersley:** Suhas Asnikar / Mangala Purushottam (br); Will Heap / Mike Rose (cra). **5 Dorling Kindersley:** Suhas Asnikar / Mangala Purushottam (tr, bc); Will Heap / John Brocklehurst (tc); Will Heap / Gavin Allen (tl); Suhas Asnikar / Mangala Purushottam (cla); Will Heap / John Brocklehurst (cra). **6 Dorling Kindersley:** Will Heap / John Pitt (cb); Chris Hornbecker / Ryan Neil (cla); Chris Hornbecker / Ryan Neil (cra); Will Heap / Peter Chan (bl). **7 Dorling Kindersley:** Suhas Asnikar / Mangala Purushottam (tl); Will Heap / John Pitt (tr); Chris Hornbecker / Ryan Neil (cb). **10 Dorling Kindersley:** Will Heap / John Pitt. **11 Dorling Kindersley:** Will Heap / Peter Chan. **18 Dorling Kindersley:** Will Heap / Peter Chan (bl). **31 Dorling Kindersley:** Will Heap / John Brocklehurst (ca). **56–57 Dorling Kindersley:** Will Heap / Mike Rose. **60–61 Dorling Kindersley:** Suhas Asnikar / Mangala Purushottam. **62–63 Dorling Kindersley:** Will Heap / Gavin Allen. **64–65 Dorling Kindersley:** Suhas Asnikar / Mangala Purushottam. **72–73 Dorling Kindersley:** Will Heap / John Brocklehurst. **78–79 Dorling Kindersley:** Suhas Asnikar / Mangala Purushottam. **80–81 Dorling Kindersley:** Suhas Asnikar / Mangala Purushottam. **82–83 Dorling Kindersley:** Will Heap / John Brocklehurst. **84–85 Dorling Kindersley:** Chris Hornbecker / Ryan Neil. **92–93 Dorling Kindersley:** Chris Hornbecker / Ryan Neil. **96–97 Dorling Kindersley:** Will Heap / Peter Chan. **102–103 Dorling Kindersley:** Will Heap / John Pitt. **110–111 Dorling Kindersley:** Chris Hornbecker / Ryan Neil. **116–117 Dorling Kindersley:** Suhas Asnikar / Mangala Purushottam. **130–131 Dorling Kindersley:** Chris Hornbecker / Ryan Neil. **135 Dorling Kindersley:** Will Heap / John Pitt

Cover images:

All other images © Dorling Kindersley
For further information see: www.dkimages.com